CONTENTS

C000077628

LIST OF TABLES

LIST OF FIGURES

LIST OF ACRONYMS AND ABBREVIATIONS

ADMADE	Administrative Design for Management (of GMAs)
CITES	Convention on International Trade in Endangered Species of Flora and Fauna
EG	Economics Group
GMA	Game Management Areas
GEMS	Global Environmental Monitoring System
IIED	International Institute for Environment and Development
ITRG	Ivory Trade Review Group
IUCN	International Union for the Conservation of Nature
LEEC	London Environmental Economics Centre
LIRDP	Luangwa Integrated Resource Development Project (Zambia)
RRAG	Renewable Resources Assessment Group
UNDP	United Nations Development Programme
UNEP	United Nations Environment Programme
WWF	Worldwide Fund for Nature

PREFACE

The plight of the African elephant has attracted extensive media attention in the last few years. This has been the result of a sustained campaign by conservationists to bring the problem to the attention of the general public, the scientific community and, most important, the governments of both African and ivory importing nations. There are few nobler and more fascinating animals than the elephant. The authors of this book are well acquainted with Africa and with the problems of wildlife conservation. Our perspective, however, is rather different from that of many (but far from all) conservationists. We believe, strongly, that economics offers an *added* dimension to the case for conservation and preservation, contrary to the popular image of economics as the despoiler of nature. We bring some of the arguments to bear in this book.

The book arose from work the authors did in 1988-9 with the Ivory Trade Review Group, an international group of experts that set out to study the existing state of the population of African elephants, trends in that population and the measures needed to control the trade in ivory. In 1989, the ITRG recommended that elephants be given an "Appendix 1" listing by the Convention on International Trade in Endangered Species (CITES), effectively an outright ban on the world ivory trade. As part of ITRG, the authors of this book agreed to the recommendation on the understanding that very clear *incentives* be given to the various nations to cooperate. As an example, southern African states generally manage their elephant populations well and on a sustainable basis. They have no incentive to participate in an outright ban. Indeed, they would lose valuable revenues. If a ban is effected, these countries at least would need compensation. In the event, CITES agreed to the ban but there is, as yet, little evidence that the incentive requirement will be implemented.

The authors' preferred option was a very limited trade in ivory, designed to maintain the incentive to sustained management in the southern African countries and to encourage other countries to follow suit. Equally, on the demand side, users of ivory would have access to albeit limited supplies, reducing the incentive to push further underground a trade that already has substantial elements of smuggling and blackmarket features. In the event, we were not successful in persuading our ITRG colleagues to accept our plan. It is understandable that the concept of an outright ban should appeal. We share the view that trading in the products of an unsustainable harvest of such beautiful and magical creatures is immoral. But some of the harvest is sustainable and, however much good it does for our consciences, the appeal to morality rarely does much in the real world of greed and commerce (which we distinguish sharply from the world of economics). Like so many other international issues, the ivory trade is a "game" in which there are many players, all with individual motives and concerns. Failure to capture those motives and concerns in an international agreement inevitably risks no agreement or its eventual breakdown. This much the theory of games teaches us. And it was this insight that we sought to build into our own proposals. For the record then, we repeat our own position in this book. We hope the ivory trade ban works. We think our solution was better and it may yet come to that if the ban fails.

But whether the reader is in or out of sympathy with our view on how the trade should be controlled, there are many other features of the book that we think are interesting. To our knowledge, our work on the economics of the trade is the first of its kind. We worked closely with the Wildlife Trade Monitoring Unit in Cambridge of the World Conservation Monitoring Centre, which is a joint venture between the three partners who developed the World Conservation Strategy: IUCN - the International Union for the Conservation of Nature, UNEP - United Nations Environment Programme, and WWF - Worldwide Fund for Nature. Without their extensive work on the trade database, none of this work would have been possible. It was a privilege to work with them, and with the many conservation experts who contributed to the ITRG. We decided to "go it alone" with this book, not out of disrespect for our colleagues - the very opposite is the case - but because we wanted the economic case to be clearly delineated and because we wanted to encourage other economists to get "on board" in the fight to save the world's wild species.

EB, JB, TS, DWP.

ACKNOWLEDGEMENTS

We are deeply indebted to the Wildlife Trade Monitoring Unit (WTMU), Cambridge, and particularly its Acting Head, Richard Luxmoore, who provided the basic customs and CITES data on the ivory trade since 1979 on which we based our analyses. The statistical expertise of WTMU in this area and their extensive work on the trade database was critical to our efforts, and we are extremely grateful.

We would also like to thank Sue Pearce for her contributions to the original research work conducted for the ITRG. Her assistance in preparing much of the basic statistics required for our analysis and her sincere interests in the plight of the African elephant are much appreciated. In the end, it is such unselfish efforts - in this case dedicated to an endangered species - which are often the backbone of a research project.

Invaluable research assistance on the worked ivory trade was also provided by Emma Penfold, to whom we are also grateful.

1 ELEPHANTS IN DECLINE

Introduction

Are elephants worth more dead than alive? This is not a trivial question. It is in fact the key economic problem that any inquiry into elephants and the ivory trade has to address. We know that the ivory harvested from elephants has a high commercial value, which is increasing as the population becomes scarce. But is this increasing scarcity and commercial value a crucial determinant of the elephants' decline in Africa, or might it also be part of the solution to conserving elephant populations? Elephants also have other values than their ivory. Elephants are one of Africa's "big five" species of large mammals that are major tourist attractions. Elephants also have an important ecological role in opening up areas for livestock and in ensuring ecological balance. On the other hand, elephants are also known to cause extensive crop and other economic damage where there are land-use conflicts between the species and human populations. Do these additional non-ivory values of elephants provide sufficient incentives for preserving the African elephant, and can we manage elephant populations so as to maximize their total economic value, including ivory values where appropriate? How does regulation of the ivory trade contribute to this *sustainable management* of elephant populations, and can we design an effective international regulatory mechanism towards this end?

This book attempts to address these questions. We recognize that there are no easy solutions. Indeed, we are only just beginning to ask the right questions and to consider that elephants and the ivory trade are an economic problem. We are unaware of any other book that examines the ivory trade, its regulation and its implications for elephant management from a truly economic perspective. Hopefully, we can make some contribution to the ongoing international debate over the future of the African elephant and the appropriate steps needed for its sustainable management.

The Decline of the African Elephant

The population of elephants in Africa has halved in eight years from 1.2 million to just over 600,000.[1] Kenya's elephant population alone has declined by two-thirds from its 1981 population of 65,000 to 16,000 in 1989. During the same period Tanzania has lost over 130,000 elephants and Zambia 128,000 – almost three-quarters of its 1981 population. Although the data presented in Table 1.1 indicate that populations have been rising in the central, forested regions of Africa, such as Gabon and Congo, this is due to improved population counts rather than rising population levels. In only a few African countries – South Africa, Botswana, Zimbabwe, Malawi and Namibia – are numbers at least stable. Population projections by the Renewable Resources Assessment Group (RRAG) at Imperial College, London in a report to the Ivory Trade Review Group

---

Table 1.1: Elephant numbers: regions and selected countries

	1981[a]	1989[b]
Zaire	376,000	112,000
CAR*	31,000	23,000
Chad	NA	2,100
Congo	10,800	42,000
Equatorial Guinea	NA	500
Gabon	13,400	74,000
Central Africa Total	436,200	277,000
Kenya	65,000	16,000
Tanzania	203,900	61,000
Sudan	133,000	22,000
Ethiopia	NA	8,000
Rwanda	150	50
Somalia	24,300	2,000
Uganda	2,300	1,600
East Africa Total	429,500	110,000
Botswana	20,000	68,000
South Africa	8,000	7,800
Zambia	160,000	32,000
Zimbabwe	47,000	52,000
Angola	12,400	18,000
Malawi	4,500	2,800
Mozambique	54,800	17,000
Nambia	2,300	32,000
Southern Africa Total	309,000	204,000

	1981[a]	*1989*[b]
Benin	1,250	2,100
Burkina Fasa	NA	4,500
Ghana	970	2,800
Guinea	800	560
Guinea Bissau	NA	40
Ivory Coast	4,800	3,600
Liberia	2,000	1,300
Mali	780	840
Mauritania	40	100
Niger	800	440
Nigeria	1,820	1,300
Senegal	200	140
Sierra Leone	500	380
Togo	150	380
West Africa Total	17,600	15,700
Africa Total	1,192,300	622,700

Note: * = Central African Republic
        NA = not available

[a] UNEP/IUCN/WWF, *Elephants and Rhinos in Africa – A Time for Decision*, (1982). Based on findings and recommendations of the African Elephant and Rhino Specialist Group.
[b] Recent estimates (October 1989) from Ian Douglas-Hamilton of the African Elephant and Rhino Specialist Group.

(ITRG) suggest that, at the rate of decline seen in 1986, elephants could be extinct by 2010.[2]

There are two species of African elephant, the bush or savannah elephant, *Loxodanta africana africana*, and the forest elephant, *L.a. cyclotis*. In the past, the impact on the forest elephant of harvesting ivory was not thought to be as significant as for the savannah elephant. Instead, human population pressure for land was considered a major population constraint. However, more recent evidence suggests that the rate of decline of the forest elephant may be similar to that of the savannah elephant, although this population reduction is more conspicious in the savannah region.[3] Thus we have now reached the stage where for all African elephants the poorly managed international trade in ivory, and the illegal hunting serving this trade, are the most significant factors in the decline of the elephant population.

There is evidence that the way in which elephants are harvested is further precipitating their population decline. The main cash value of the elephant is its tusks, although the hide is also demanded both internationally and locally, and the meat is often consumed locally. Poaching has seriously disrupted breeding patterns in some herds because gunmen pick off elephants with big tusks, typically the older and more sexually active males. In Tanzania's Mikumi reserve, where poachers are very active, the ratio was 99.6 per cent females to 0.4 per cent males. Populations in Queen Elizabeth Park in Uganda and Tsavo in Kenya are similarily skewed. An elephant cow is fertile for only two days during her three-monthly oestrus, and must find a rutting male during this brief period. The chances of mating successfully under these conditions are slim. What is more, with the male populations decimated, poachers turn their attentions to the smaller tusked females. Studies in Amboseli National Park, Kenya show that for every adult female elephant killed at least one immature elephant will die. A calf younger than two years old stands no chance of surviving the death of its mother, while a calf orphaned between two and five years old has a 30 per cent chance of survival, and one aged between six and ten years old has a 48 per cent chance of survival.[4]

This dramatic decline in elephant numbers in most of Africa has been largely attributed to illegal harvesting, i.e. poaching of elephants for ivory. In recent years, poaching and the decline of the African elephant have become synonymous in the public mind. However, the situation is more complicated than that.

The Role of the Ivory Trade

Set against this population decline, the historical trend in the international ivory trade has been one of sustained growth from 1945 through the mid-1980s – from 204 tonnes of raw (i.e. unworked) elephant ivory in 1950 to 412 tonnes in 1960, 564 tonnes in 1970 and around 1,000 tonnes in 1980. This represents a greater than 400 per cent increase in the trade in ivory over 40 years, or over 10 per cent per annum each year for the four past decades. Best estimates of the trade occurring in the last decade are given in Table 1.2. Up to 1986, records indicate that between 700 and 1,000 tonnes of raw ivory were traded internationally each year.

As shown in Figure 1.1, the price of ivory has been increasing dramatically: between 1979 and 1985 the current price of one kilogram of ivory was around $60, in 1987 it reached over $120 and in early 1989 it rose towards $300 per kilogram. Thus the ivory trade

**Figure 1.1: Implicit current ivory prices, 1979–88
(unweighted average, US$/kg)**

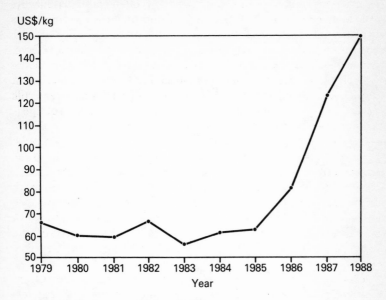

Source: London Environmental Economics Centre.

is a highly lucrative activity. (All prices are given in US dollars unless otherwise stated.)

Table 1.2 shows that the sum total of ivory exported between 1979 and 1988 amounts to between 7,624,882 and 7,954,544 kg (see also Chapter 2). As a very approximate guide it can be taken that an average pair of tusks weighs 9–10 kg (although this is a dangerous assumption as average tusk weights have changed over time) and from this it can be estimated that during this period between 700,000 and 800,000 elephants were exploited for their ivory.

The decline in tonnage since 1979 looks encouraging, but the statistics hide the real impact of the ivory trade on the elephant population. In 1979 one tonne of ivory represented approximately 54 dead elephants. These were mainly the bull elephants, valued for their bigger tusks, with an average tusk weight per elephant of 9.3 kg. By 1987 most of the mature bull elephants had been shot, leaving cows and calves to support the demand for ivory. They have a much lower average tusk size of 4.7 kg, such that one tonne of ivory now

Table 1.2: Volume of African raw ivory exports, 1979–88 (kg)

	1979	1980	1981	1982	1983	1984
Angola	0	0	5	0	50	10
Benin	0	0	0	195	0	0
Botswana	12,699	5,494	8,750	4,689	5,580	3,648
Burkina	0	0	35	26	0	0
Burundi	138,880	125,733	61,009	46,416	124,340	183,989
Cameroon	7,331	7,870	2,195	2,613	869	1,896
CAR	181,233	182,660	107,164	201,695	203,852	121,592
Chad	27,017	4,200	13,456	27,594	33,743	4,383
Congo	93,158	175,499	236,784	101,968	53,499	95,302
I. Coast	701	1,078	1,090	14,713	559	351
Djibouti	0	0	0	0	0	0
Egypt	0	0	30	0	10	0
Ethiopia	0	0	0	00	0	172
Gabon	3,746	1,482	1,107	239	874	223
Ghana	500	28	80	112	15	30
Guinea	0	10	0	0	15	0
Kenya	45,703	30,198	5,642	12,399	4,012	12,883
Liberia	90	105	0	10	17	4
Malawi	560	2	735	263	1,191	329
Mali	0	0	0	0	0	0
Mozambique	5,949	714	10	870	16	960
Namibia	22,005	1,754	152	5,683	1,642	3,040
Niger	0	0	0	0	0	0
Nigeria	210	640	522	420	273	162
Rwanda	0	170	80	0	0	0
S. Africa	41,950	35,198	32,198	28,438	45,519	36,256
Senegal	0	273	89	0	1	6
S. Leone	0	48	29	10	5	0
Somalia	0	108	18,240	7,468	852	7,247
Sudan	124,438	205,626	268,579	278,329	337,317	67,909
Swaziland	0	0	0	0	0	0
Tanzania	33,283	44,963	26,738	17,515	15,464	44,824
Togo	0	200	20	0	50	160
Uganda	25,471	19,292	45,125	12,268	12,702	99,547
Zaire	160,247	84,399	45,256	78,299	157,084	90,199
Zambia	15,551	22,452	28,023	33,957	18,308	1,659
Zimbabwe	3,030	1,650	1,303	14,147	14,075	20,814
Min. Total	943,752	951,846	905,075	890,336	1,031,934	797,595
Maximum						
Burundi	144,880	189,783	61,478	46,416	132,124	183,989
Sudan	124,438	354,112	275,279	288,329	337,317	67,909
Max. Total	949,752	1,164,382	912,244	900,336	1,039,718	797,595

Note: These are the "best estimates" of African exports, disaggregated by country of export, using import and export data from customs sources, and CITES data. Both *legal* and *illegal* exports are likely to be included. For starred years (*), because of the adoption of the Management Quota System by CITES, there may have been an incentive to evade both customs and CITES systems in some countries. (CAR: Central African Republic)

	1985	1986*	1987*	1988*	Total
Angola	0	0	0	0	65
Benin	10	0	0	0	205
Botswana	16,519	360	371	65	58,175
Burkina	20	0	0	0	81
Burundi	215,218	138,159	50,270	8,655	1,092,669
Cameroon	1,591	805	3,132	2,538	30,840
CAR	116,624	19,367	2,070	260	1,136,517
Chad	38	0	1,606	0	112,037
Congo	72,280	17,058	86,377	18,806	950,731
I. Coast	454	137	491	988	20,562
Djibouti	0	0	0	10,901	10,901
Egypt	3	5	0	0	48
Ethiopia	6,193	4,600	1,764	2,160	14,889
Gabon	372	481	4,212	13,542	26,278
Ghana	0	70	75	0	910
Guinea	5	0	0	0	30
Kenya	18,733	1,787	143	0	131,500
Liberia	25	21	26	0	298
Malawi	830	79	958	762	5,709
Mali	0	5	3	0	8
Mozambique	860	1,597	6,336	7,302	24,614
Namibia	1,837	1,268	1	0	37,382
Niger	0	0	18	0	18
Nigeria	232	92	0	6,000	8,551
Rwanda	4,485	3,224	0	0	7,959
S. Africa	49,545	40,935	17,723	7,557	335,948
Senegal	55	0	30	0	454
S. Leone	10	0	0	0	102
Somalia	4,508	64,413	4,819	0	107,655
Sudan	22,116	77,706	69,579	0	1,451,599
Swaziland	276	0	0	0	276
Tanzania	113,968	301,838	56,374	42,581	697,548
Togo	170	90	135	0	825
Uganda	206,353	3,104	4	281	424,147
Zaire	21,852	22,899	11,853	11,009	683,097
Zambia	14,454	11,038	4,325	1,622	151,389
Zimbabwe	22,824	7,946	8,093	6,983	100,865
Min. Total	912,460	719,084	330,788	142,012	7,624,882
Maximum					
Burundi	215,218	224,332	50,270	8,655	1,248,490
Sudan	22,116	77,706	69,579	0	1,616,785
Max. Total	912,460	805,257	330,788	142,012	7,954,544

Source: The data were compiled by Richard Luxmoore from the Wildlife Trade Monitoring Unit for *The Ivory Trade and the Future of the African Elephant*, Report of the Ivory Trade Review Group, prepared for the second meeting of the CITES African Elephant Working Group, (Gabarone, Botswana, July 1989).

directly represents about 113 dead elephants. There is a further disturbing indirect effect that needs to be considered. The high female ratio of the harvested population leads to the death of a further 55 calves with no ivory, who are orphaned or die of starvation. As a consequence, almost the same number of elephants were harvested in 1987 (when about 370 tonnes were in the trade) as in 1979 (when nearly 1,000 tonnes were in the trade), but from a much reduced and more fragile population.

Where has all this ivory been consumed? There are two different aspects to this question. First, there is the movement of ivory to the carving centres of the trade – these are the nations which are the "manufacturers of worked ivory" and the "consumers of raw ivory". Second, there is the movement of ivory in international trade to the final holders of ivory – these are the nations which are the "final consumers of worked ivory".

The carving centres in the international trade have traditionally been Hong Kong and Japan, with an average consumption of 40 per cent and 30 per cent respectively. Europe once had a viable carving industry, which is no longer of significance. Africa internal carving is the next most significant consumer of raw ivory. After carving, ivory is most often re-exported to the final consuming states. The only exception is Japan, which is both a substantial carver and consumer of ivory. Ivory is a precious primary commodity which commands an international price in hard currency. In addition, quality handcrafting of this fine material also generates hard currency.

The flow of ivory in international trade has generally been toward the hard currency consumers – the USA, Europe and, more recently, Japan. These three consumers have acquired about 75 per cent of all ivory worked in Hong Kong and Japan this decade (see Chapter 3). The remainder of the ivory in international trade has been utilized in the carving industries within various developing countries – India, China – and then re-exported, or sold to tourists for hard currency. The same is true for much of African worked ivory. Therefore, it is very likely that nearly all of the ivory in the international trade has ultimately found its way to one of the three hard currency consumers: the USA, Europe and Japan.

The primary cause of the growth in the ivory trade may be traced to the ivory's character as a precious material, used in sculpture and jewellery. These items are heavily demanded in times of income growth – and the era since 1945 has been one of significant income growth worldwide, particularly in Japan.

Ivory has been a culturally demanded substance in Asia for several centuries. In Japan the ivory is especially prized for making *hankos*,

Table 1.3: Net imports of raw ivory by major consumers, 1979-88 (tonnes)

	1979	1980	1981	1982	1983	1984	1985	1986*	1987*	1988*
USA	6	23	11	7	20	55	24	17	21	9
FR Germany	74	181	32	35	43	-7	16	7	2	1
UK	-5	-26	0	-3	2	3	28	-1	7	3
Hong Kong	366	376	427	318	428	267	109	129	150	133
India	17	19	19	24	23	30	21	8	6	4
France	89	22	7	4	11	21	5	5	4	-2
China	7	10	10	54	20	7	7	19	39	50
Japan	270	240	256	205	174	179	206	29	103	75
Thailand	1	1	2	4	-5	-12	-2	1	0	-3
Belgium	16	-90	-248	-123	-105	-116	0	0	-10	12
Singapore	-7	-4	3	7	0	120	60	324	-148	-129
Taiwan	11	18	17	18	28	34	21	18	80	5
Macau	–	0	0	5	16	38	82	57	8	11
Total Net Imports, All Countries (Min. estimate)	979	967	895	891	1,018	710	749	600	370	153

Note: These "best estimates" of final demand for raw ivory by the main consuming countries are based on customs trade statistics and CITES documentation, and were compiled by the London Environmental Economics Centre, based on data provided by the Wildlife Trade Monitoring Unit, Cambridge.

Minus figures indicate that countries were *net exporters* in that year, most likely through destocking.

For starred years (*), because of the adoption of the Management Quota System by CITES, there may have been an incentive to evade both customs and CITES systems in some countries.

personal seals traditionally used by some Japanese in place of a signature. The rapid post-war economic development of Japan and other Asian countries has translated into an increased purchasing power for importing ivory. Tables 1.3 and 1.4 show that the major demand for raw and worked ivory since 1979 has been in East Asia, especially Japan and more recently Singapore (see also Chapter 3). Over the past 25 years, for every doubling of Japanese incomes, net imports of raw ivory have increased by 150 per cent or more (see Chapter 4). Consequently, between 1960 and 1985, as world consumption of unworked ivory increased by 100 per cent (412 tonnes to 780 tonnes), Japanese consumption increased by 200 per cent (150 tonnes to 422 tonnes).

Therefore, one of the impacts of economic development in Asia (as represented by Japan's leading example) has been to produce a

Table 1.4: Net imports of raw and worked ivory by major consumers, 1979–88

Net imports of raw ivory by major consumers
(% of total)

	1979	1980	1981	1982	1983	1984	1985	1986	1987	1988
Hong Kong	37	39	48	36	40	38	15	22	40	86
Japan	28	25	32	29	20	30	27	5	28	49
EEC	18	12	5	5	6	4	6	2	1	9
USA	1	3	1	1	2	8	3	3	6	6
Taiwan	2	2	2	2	3	3	3	3	22	3
Macau	0	0	0	0	2	4	11	10	2	7
China	1	1	1	7	2	0	1	3	10	32
India	2	2	2	3	2	3	3	1	2	3
Singapore	(−1)	0	0	1	0	17	8	54	(−40)	(−84)
Thailand	0	0	0	0	0	(−2)	0	0	0	(−2)

Source: Table 1.3.

Net imports of worked ivory by major consumers
(% of total, 1979–84 average)

Japan	38
EEC	18
USA	16
Other Asian	3
(Singapore, Taiwan, S. Korea and Macau)	

Source: London Environmental Economics Centre, based on 1979–84 data from Japan and Hong Kong. The trade from these two countries is likely to comprise 75 per cent of the total worked ivory trade.

---

substantial demand for elephant ivory. It is apparent that this latent demand for ivory exists in a number of other Asian states – such as Korea and Taiwan, where demand has increased by 1,000 per cent in the past decade – and that demand pressures will remain high so long as economic growth continues at a rapid pace in this region, as it appears it will for a long time to come.

Other rapidly developing countries, such as Singapore, Dubai and Macau, have been playing an increasingly important role in the movement of raw ivory stocks and in their processing and carving. This fluidity is one of the characteristics of both the legal and illegal trade: whenever one channel through which ivory is passing has been blocked, another has opened up almost immediately. The entrance of new countries into the ivory trade and its fluidity are important issues to be tackled by any regime of international regulation (see Chapters 5 and 6).

The Economics of the Decline in Elephant Populations

People harvest ivory in order to make money. In investing time and effort in hunting elephants, individuals are essentially comparing the returns from this activity to alternative sources of income available to them. If the *relative* returns from harvesting ivory are high, then clearly this will be the preferred activity. Unfortunately, even if elephants may be regarded as an important source of *income*, they may still not be regarded as a valuable *asset* to be sustainably managed and maintained.

If elephants are considered a valuable asset, i.e. a source of wealth that increases in value over time, then it may be worthwhile to maintain elephants into the future to take advantage of this increasing value. However, there are other assets, or forms of wealth, in the economy that yield income. The comparable returns from these assets will determine the general *rate of interest* in the economy. The existence of these alternative investment opportunities means that, for example, £1 invested in these assets today may in a year's time be worth £1.10. This implies a 10 per cent rate of interest. It also implies that we would be giving up at least this amount of earnings for every £1 invested in maintaining elephant populations. Thus, one way of comparing the relative returns of maintaining elephants would be to apply a *discount rate* of 10 per cent to this future income stream.

In practice, the rate at which we discount the future value of maintaining elephants will depend not only on the opportunity cost of capital, as just implied, but also on *individuals' time preference*. That is, people may be reluctant to wait for future returns from maintaining elephants because they are simply impatient for money now, because of uncertainty over the future, including a high risk of death, and because improving incomes mean that additional wealth in the future is less valuable than it is today.

In most African countries, the relationships between ivory prices, the costs of harvesting and the return on comparable investments – as reflected in the interest or discount rate – are such that exploiters of elephant ivory may be content with only short-term profits. The result will be over-exploitation of elephants, as is evident at present.

In terms of the economic theory of renewable resources, we can therefore suggest an economic interpretation of the decline in elephant numbers. The theory tells us that if we have a combination of:

(a) a high ratio of the price of ivory to the cost of harvesting (poaching), and
(b) a high discount rate by users relative to the growth rate of the elephant population,

then, from the standpoint of the exploiter, it is actually optimal to run the resource down, even to extinction. The basic bioeconomic model illustrating these conditions is developed in Appendix 1.1. These conditions are clearly present with African elephants.

Condition (a) suggests that the existence of excessive *economic rent*, or *surplus profit*, from ivory will provide an incentive towards over-harvesting elephants. In economics, rent is the difference between the total value of selling a commodity and the costs of supplying it. Thus, rent can in principle be determined by deducting from the gross income earned the cost of labour, materials and capital inputs (including the costs of paying a normal return, or profit, to capital). The existence of rent therefore implies more remuneration than is required to keep an activity in operation – hence, the term "surplus profit". If large rents are available from, say, ivory harvesting, then there will be an incentive for many individuals to undertake this activity, or alternatively, for the individuals already exploiting ivory to expand their activities.

Poaching is not costless but it is cheap, relative to the price of ivory, leading to sizeable rents. The individuals involved in the actual illegal hunting are often very poor and are paid rates just marginally better than prevailing rural wages. Even if the entire poaching operation is highly organized and well equipped with modern weaponry, vehicles and communications, these costs may be easily recovered by the high value of tusks. Basically, the mobility and effectiveness of modernized operations means that more elephants can be killed, reducing significantly the per unit costs of poaching the tusks. As noted, the price of ivory is buoyant because of strong final demand for worked and unworked ivory in Asian consuming countries. Condition (a) is thus met, and the high rents provide the incentive for illegal harvesting to take place.

However, condition (a) alone is not sufficient to cause over-exploitation of elephant populations. As will be discussed below, this condition may actually be an incentive for African governments to engage in sustainable management of their elephant populations – provided that they can capture a sufficient proportion of the rents that would otherwise go to poachers or external traders. Thus it is not the mere existence of rents from ivory harvesting but who captures these rents which often determines the incentives for over-exploitation.

Condition (b) needs to be modified to allow for changes in the real price of ivory over time. It is this condition which dictates whether elephants are considered by individuals to be a valuable asset worth maintaining. As elephant populations increase in numbers, the standing crop of ivory is also increasing. Other factors also affect the quantity of ivory produced, such as the age structure and male-female ratio of the population, as well as the degree to which it is stressed by over-hunting, by changing environmental conditions and space/food constraints. But on the whole, if elephants are maintained as an investment, then future ivory returns are determined by the population growth rate plus any appreciations in the real value of ivory. Basically, if the population growth rate is less than the net effective discount rate (actual discount rates less the rate of the real price increase) it will be optimal to the exploiter to run the resource down to extinction (see Appendix 1.1).

For example, if the natural rate of population increase is 3 per cent per year and real ivory values are increasing at 5 per cent annually, the total increase in value would still be less than the returns on other assets, if the discount rate is above 8 per cent. Again, this implies that it is more profitable to harvest elephants completely today and re-invest the returns in alternative assets; or alternatively, it may imply that individuals would rather have the income from ivory today than wait for it to increase in value. Although if real prices grow faster through time they will slow the rate of exploitation, it only takes a significantly higher discount rate relative to the growth rate for condition (b) to be met. Compared to many other species, the growth rate of elephant populations is low – around 6 per cent under favourable conditions.[5] It is likely that discount rates in most African countries are considerably higher, both because of high opportunity costs of capital and high rates of time preference.

Given this slow rate of growth, it may be the case that investments in elephants under existing conditions cannot yield a competitive return. However, there are at least two major reasons for suggesting that what is actually happening at present to elephant populations is not socially desirable.

First, the costs of elephant harvesting incurred by the individual harvester may not include the wider social costs. These may include: the loss to the relevant populations of sustainable future income from ivory and other elephant products (the "user cost" argument); the loss of any ecological and tourist values (the "external cost" argument); and the loss of existence value to people who simply want elephants to be conserved. (For more on the total economic value of elephants, see "Economic incentives for conservation", p. 17.) All of these costs may be significant, but they may also be offset somewhat by some savings from mortality, e.g. foregone elephant-damage costs, such as crop damages and woodland destruction. However, since the price of ivory does not reflect the full cost of elephant offtake, the level of supply and demand of ivory, and consequently the rate of decline in elephant population levels, is not socially desirable.

Second, the discount rates of ivory consumers, traders and poachers are likely to be above socially determined discount rates. The arguments for supposing this to be the case are many.[6] Essentially, institutional failings and uncertainties contribute to these excessively high discount rates, and these factors are discussed at greater length in Chapter 5.

Finally, there is an additional reason for supposing that the level of elephant harvesting is not optimal. Elephants (where left insufficiently protected) are being treated as open-access resources. Economic theory tells us that such resources will be used by people up to the point where the total costs of utilizing them equals the total revenues, i.e. to the point where rents (profits) are driven to zero. While this situation may be stable, it implies a high risk of over-use and under-investment with regard to these forms of resources. Thus, a number of different factors point in the direction that the current decline in elephant numbers is economically unwarranted.

Further Issues in the Decline of Elephant Populations

Three further issues must be considered in any analysis of the decline in elephant populations:

(i)   the competition for land;
(ii) the dissipation of rent and rent capture; and
(iii) the conditions leading to high discount rates in rural Africa.

Competition for land

The competing for land argument embraces Hardin's notion of the survival of the fittest, where the demands of two sympathetic species are sufficiently similar that competition between them leads to the extinction of one.[7] In this case, the species are humans and elephants, who compete for essential resources of food and habitat. Humans' plant foods demands are similar to those of the elephant, and they also indirectly compete for the use of the same resources for their domestic stock. This competition is likely to be significant, given that the African population doubling-time is now merely 18 years, and has brought about rapid forest conversion for agricultural and pastoral activity.

Rent dissipation and capture

As noted in the previous section, the decision whether to maintain the stock of elephants or convert this population to an alternative form of asset – in this case ivory – is affected by the dissipation and capture of rents derived from elephants.[8] (Here, rents are taken to be the difference between the value received from the final sale of ivory and the cost of initially harvesting the ivory.) In the case of the African elephant, rents from the sale of elephant ivory are *dispersed* across a wide range of individuals, including poachers, local traders, local chieftains, domestic officials, foreign traders and so on. The individual who actually makes the harvesting decision receives a relatively insignificant proportion of the total revenue (and thus receives relatively low returns from the resource, compared to the actual returns accruing to the resource) upon which to base his consumption/investment decision. In addition, the putative ''owners'' of the resource (e.g. the state game and parks departments) often only receive a very small share of the resource rents, usually from the sale of confiscated ivory.

Ivory rents are *dissipated* by virtue of such wide and diverse dispersion. There is also great uncertainty and risk involved in abstaining from current conversion in order to generate a flow of revenue from the resource in the future. Dissipation of rents, uncertainty and risk all combine to create an incentive to harvest ivory as quickly as possible. The following figures give some indication of the sums that accrue to harvesters in Africa compared to the value of raw ivory in Japan.

Table 1.5: Revenues flowing to harvesters in Africa and Comparison with raw ivory value in Japan, 1985[9]

Chad	CAR	Cameroon	Zaire	Zimbabwe	Japan
$7/kg	$6–8/kg	$15/kg	$7/kg	$63–76/kg	$85–99/kg

Note: CAR refers to Central African Republic

The difference between the ivory revenues from Zimbabwe and those of the other African countries has to do with management strategies. Unlike the other states, the Zimbabwean government in the 1980s actively managed, culled and marketed ivory precisely to capture as large a proportion of the rents from ivory as possible (see

Chapters 5 and 6). Although perhaps a bit on the high side, Zimbabwean sale revenues are therefore a good indicator of the gross sale value of ivory that could be received in Africa.

Details on the cost of harvesting ivory are not known; however, as an illustration it is reasonable to assume that Zimbabwean harvesters receive a competitive wage which approximates to about $5/kg of all the ivory harvested. This would suggest that the state is receiving around $60/kg in actual rents from the resource. If Japan is taken as the point of final sale, then the total rents available would be at most $85/kg ($85–99/kg less the $5/kg cost of harvesting). Thus *rent capture* by Zimbabwe is high – at least 70 per cent. In comparison, the rent capture by the other African countries represented in Table 1.5 is extremely low, with the remainder of available rents captured by external traders.

What is more, the vast diversity of the rent receivers, with the majority of rents typically flowing to foreign traders, makes it virtually impossible for all rent receivers to come together to manage the resource effectively. Elephant management is instead left solely to the governments of those countries with elephants. However, as noted above, these states have generally failed to capture sufficient rent from the ivory trade to make adequate elephant management proposals worthwhile, including monitoring, protection and harvesting controls. This is reflected in the relatively insignificant investment in elephant protection. In the last ten years, elephant range areas have shrunk by 20 per cent from 7.3 million km^2 to 5.9 million km^2, and of these only 1.5 per cent are strictly wardened and adequately protected.[10]

The existence of high rents – in the above example around $85/kg – indicates a strong incentive to harvest ivory, but the failure of African states to capture a large proportion of these rents means that there is little incentive to protect and manage elephant populations. The result is high levels of exploitation through illegal harvesting.

Conditions leading to high discount rates

As discussed in the section on "The decline of the African elephant" (p. 2), high discount rates are a disincentive for individuals to consider elephants as a valuable long-term investment, regardless of the high current value of ivory. There are several reasons why individuals' discount rates may be extremely high in rural Africa.

First, many rural populations in Africa are faced with a *high opportunity cost of capital*. Although base lending rates throughout sub-Saharan Africa are around 10–15 per cent,[11] formal credit markets are non-existent in many rural areas. Because of the vast poverty in these areas, the level of savings generated is also low. Thus capital is scarce, and what finance is available for investment is from informal sources, e.g. moneylenders, advances in lieu of production, crop sharing and so forth. Informal lending rates can be around 50–100 per cent, but may even be much higher. Such high rates of interest discourage any investment by rural populations that involve short-term sacrifices for the sake of future gains.[12] Thus, relatively slow growing investments, such as elephant ivory, are relatively unattractive. When surplus money is available it is invested in activities that can yield more immediate benefits, such as material goods for a store, social goods such as gift giving for expected support, livestock and land for agricultural production.[13]

Rural people in Africa may also have a *high time rate of preference*. that is, they are likely to prefer having income in the present as opposed to the future. In Africa, average life expectancy at birth is 51 years and infant mortality is 10 per cent.[14] These figures are even more grim in rural areas where health care, nutrition, education and clean water and sanitation are scarce. Thus risk of death is a crucial factor. Uncertainty of the future is also compounded by threats of drought and other natural disasters, political instability and warfare, economic disruptions and policy changes and natural resource degradation. Finally, poverty itself may force individuals to have a high rate of time preference: under conditions of extreme poverty, a household's major concern is securing sufficient means for survival today. Some observers suggest that all these conditions leading to a high rate of time preference are reflected in the lack of sustainable farming practices (practices which conserve soil quality, irrigation water and rainfall) in sub-Saharan Africa. This implies that individuals are not willing to bear the risk and uncertainty from changing farming patterns in order to benefit from future gains.[15]

Economic Incentives for Conservation

So far, we have discussed whether or not the value from ivory will provide incentives for preserving the African elephant. However, elephants have other values aside from their ivory. Some of these other values may actually provide additional incentives for preserving, rather than depleting, elephant populations. The economic incentives for conservation are therefore determined by the *sum total of economic values* of the elephant. These can be categorized into

  i)   the direct use;
 ii)   the indirect use; and
iii)   the non-use/preservation of the African elephant.[16]

Direct use value

The direct use value is derived from economic use of the resource and its services, such as for ivory or tourism. Other direct uses, such as providing meat, may be important locally but not for international trade. One argument for conservation is that it would permit a sustainable offtake of revenue from harvesting the resource (ivory, hide and meat) and from its non-consumptive economic value (tourism). This would benefit the immediate and long-term balance of payments of Africa. The alternative, to "mine" the elephant population, as is currently happening, permits short-term financial gain at the expense of sustainable income over long periods.

The sustainable management approach should more obviously appeal to exporting nations than the mining approach. In practice, however, there appears to be a preference for the short-term mining option. At a purely financial level, mining makes sense if it yields a current revenue higher than the value that would be obtained by managing the resource sustainably. How sensible it is to mine elephants on this very narrow criterion will then depend (as discussed in the section on the economics of the decline in elephant populations, p. 11) upon discount rates, expected interest rates and expected future values of ivory. It has not been feasible to engage in such an analysis, but it is possible to say how much Africa might be able to receive by way of revenue from ivory exports.

From Figure 1.1 and Table 1.2 we estimate the aggregate value of current annual ivory exports to be between $50–60 million. However, as discussed in Chapter 2, the actual export earnings for Africa are probably closer to $35–45 million. This amount is a tiny fraction of all African exports, and although significant for a few individual countries, the loss of these ivory revenues would not severely impair African development. Furthermore, other values of the African elephant, such as its importance for tourism in some countries, may be considerably more significant in terms of foreign exchange earnings. For example, in a report entitled *The Viewing Value of Elephants*, Gardner Brown and Wes Henry have attempted to estimate part of the non-consumed value of elephants.[17] Kenya is visited by about 250,000 to 300,000 foreign adult tourists annually. Based on survey responses from questionnaires filled in by safari tourists and tour operaters in Kenya, the non-transportation cost of safaris averaged $1,400. This represents potential expenditures of around $375 million, of which about $200 million is spent in Kenya. To estimate from this expenditure the actual viewing value of elephants, Brown applied travel cost and contingent valuation techniques. The results of the two techniques are quite comparable, and suggest the value of viewing elephants in Kenya to be $25 million per year. This may be as much as ten times the value of its poached ivory exports. This suggests that there is a powerful financial case for keeping elephants alive for their non-consumptive value rather than harvesting them for their ivory.

Indirect use value
Indirect use value is derived from the natural ecological functions of the elephant, such as their ability to diversify savanna and forest ecosystems, act as seed dispersers, reduce bushlands, expand grasslands and reduce the incidence of the tsetse fly. Elephants have an essential ecological role in the African savannas and forests. In a report for the Ivory Trade Review Group (ITRG), Western notes how elephants, acting as "keystone species", open up areas to make them accessible to other herbivores, including domestic stock, by feeding and trampling down tall sedges and promoting the growth of higher-quality grasses.[18]

The ecological benefits of elephants are dependent on their population density being neither too high nor too low. At each of these two extremes habitat impoverishment results, for example, in the protected areas where elephants crowd in, or the areas of non-protected lands that are abandoned. In Amboseli National Park, Kenya, there are extremely high densities of elephants in the centre of the national park, falling away to negligible levels beyond the park boundaries. The elephant density gradient is reflected in the damage to the dominant woodland tree, the yellow-barked acacia, *Acacia xanthopholoea*. During the period 1950–89 there was little change in the tree densities in the early decades, but in the late 1980s, following the compression of the elephant population in the park, the woodlands have disappeared in the park vicinity and increased in areas where elephant activity is negligible.

Both the number of plant species and their relative abundance have been similarly affected. Relatively few plants, dominated by one or two species, are located in areas of little elephant disturbance. This species richness increases in terms of species abundance and distribution in areas of the park where elephants are in moderate density. However, in the central park, where elephant densitites are exceptionally high, there is a small variety of plants with just a few dominant species. Also, where elephant densities are high, there tends to be a significant increase in grazer biomass (zebra, wildebeest, Thomson's gazelle and buffalo) and decrease in browser and mixed feeder biomass (giraffe, impala, Grant's gazelle). The reverse is true in areas where elephant densities are low. The most equitable mix of grazers and browsers is found in the mosaic of woodlands and grasslands associated with moderate elephant densities straddling the park boundaries.

The local community may also derive other indirect benefits from the elephants, such as employment from the tourist trade, a market for handicrafts and so on which could be significant. However, these indirect benefits may be offset by any detrimental crop or other damage caused by the elephant.

Non-use and preservation values
Finally, non-use values (no direct/indirect benefit from services or components) and preservation values (values in addition to direct/indirect current use) need to be considered. These embrace existence values, bequest values and option values.

Existence value is where people derive satisfaction from just knowing that elephants will be preserved. For example, it could be said that the majority of supporters of ''save the elephant'' campaigns in Western countries may never actually travel to Africa to see elephants, but they nevertheless value the existence of the African elephant. Their willingness to pay for this value is somewhat reflected in the time and money they spend on these campaigns.

The *bequest value* arises when an individual has no intention of ''using'' the elephant, but values the opportunity of future generations using them. Again, one of the strong arguments in elephant-saving campaigns is that the African elephant is one of the world's unique mammals that should be preserved in its natural habitat for future generations.

Option value is a special type of preservation value, which essentially involves individuals deciding that preservation is necessary today in order to have the option of future uses of the resource. For example, one rationale for preserving elephants may be that potentially there could be future tourist values or revenues to be gained from managed culling. Substantial, irreversible decimation of a country's elephant population carries the high risk that these future values will be lost. If society is risk-averse, the option value attached to preservation effectively insures against the risk today of irreversibly losing these future values derived from elephants. Although it is very difficult to measure and assess non-use/preservation values, this does not make them any less important than others which are financially measurable. Indeed, these values may be highly significant, both to Africans and people in the rest of the world. Moreover, if the African elephant population continues to decline – in the economist's language "become increasingly scarce" – one can expect non-use and preservation values to increase.

Current Situation

The Convention on the International Trade in Endangered Species of Flora and Fauna (CITES) was established in the early 1970s to control the trade in species threatened with extinction (see Chapter 5). CITES developed a system to control trade in listed species of flora and fauna. Specifically there are three appendices upon which any species can be listed, given the vote of the Conference of the Parties to CITES. In general, to trade in a species listed in the Appendices to the Convention, it is necessary to obtain permission from the exporting state's management authority.

Appendix I entails a ban on the international trade in the listed species for "primarily commercial purposes".

Appendix II involves no restriction on international trade, but rather requires that all such trade should be reported to the Secretariat in Annual Reports.

Appendix III is again a notification device. In this case, any state is allowed to unilaterally list a species when its domestic restrictions are more strict than the international.

The African elephant was originally listed under Appendix II of the Convention at the initial Conference of the Parties in 1976. However, this was found to be insufficient in controlling the trade in ivory. In 1985, the Appendix II listing was backed by a Management Quota System, which attempted to ensure that trade in elephant products was only allowed within the context of planned domestic management programmes..

However, populations continued to decline dramatically. At the Seventh Conference of the Parties to CITES in 1989, the African elephant was transferred up from Appendix II to Appendix I (see Chapter 6). This effectively bans all trade in elephant products; although, in future, individual countries with healthy elephant populations, an effective elephant conservation and management programme and effective ivory trade controls will be able to apply to a technical committee (yet to be established) to have the elephant populations transferred back to Appendix II listing. It was also agreed that the international trade ban should apply to all existing ivory stocks, with no special exemptions for the large ivory stockpiles – in particular in Hong Kong and Burundi. Elephant trophy imports into the USA from countries taking a reservation (see p. 133) will also be prohibited.

The CITES ban received support from the majority of the African nations and consuming countries, some of whom had already banned ivory trading domestically, for example, Kenya, the USA and Europe. However, some elephant range states and ivory consuming states voiced dissatisfaction with the proposal. Zimbabwe, Botswana, South Africa, Malawi and Zambia refused to agree to the CITES resolution to move the African elephant from Appendix II to Appendix I. Of the major consuming countries, China and Hong Kong have also declared reservations against the ban and have continued trading in African elephant ivory. This has left the international situation in a state of confusion; more importantly, it has also left the African elephant at risk while this situation continues.

Appendix 1.1: A Bioeconomic Model of Elephant Decline

Using the standard logistic function employed in renewable resource economics and bioeconomic models,[19] it can be easily shown how economic variables can influence estimates of the change in population and interpretation of its causes. The logistic function is:

$$
\begin{aligned}
dX/dt &= \text{growth } less \text{ yield} \\
&= F(X) - h \\
&= rX(1 - X/K) - qEX,
\end{aligned}
\tag{1}
$$

where X is the size of population (standing ivory crop in this case), r is its intrinsic growth, K its carrying capacity, E the level of effort and q an "effort" parameter.

However, harvesting of ivory is an economic activity which the harvesters undertake to earn a net return:

$$
\begin{aligned}
R(X,E) &= ph - c(X)E \\
&= pqEX - c(X)E,
\end{aligned}
\tag{2}
$$

where p is the price of harvested ivory and c is the unit cost of harvesting effort, which is a non-increasing function of X. If economic returns, or profits, are maximized with respect to harvesting effort, then (2) becomes:

$$
dR/dE = pqX - c(X) = 0
$$
or
$$
X = c(X)/pq .
\tag{3}
$$

Substituting (3) into (1):

$$dX/dt = [r/q(1 - X/K) - E]c(X)/p, \tag{4}$$

which suggests that an increase in ivory prices will contribute to a depletion in standing stock, whereas an increase in harvesting costs should increase the stock.

As (2) is an income stream that the exploiter seeks to maximize over time, the prevailing interest rate used in discounting future returns is also an important determinant of the harvesting rate and thus dX/dt. As we shall see, it is also crucial to determining whether the exploiter will deplete the elephant population to extinction.

From (2) and (3), the objective to be maximized over time is:

$$\max_{h} \int_0^\infty e^{-\delta t} R(X,E)\, dt = \int_0^\infty e^{-\delta t}[p - c(X)]h\, dt, \tag{5}$$

$$\text{s.t.} \qquad X(t) \geqslant 0,$$
$$h(t) \geqslant 0,$$
$$\dot{X} = F(X) - h.$$

The necessary conditions for solving this problem lead to the following equation for an optimal level of elephant stock, X^*:

$$F'(X) - \frac{c'(X)F(X)}{p - c(X)} = \delta, \tag{6}$$

where $F'(X)$ is the marginal productivity (growth) of the elephant population, and $c'(X)F(X)/p - c(X)$ is the marginal stock effort, which is negative. Thus the optimal population level, X^*, is greater than the level corresponding to the simple marginal productivity rule $F'(X) = \delta$. The increase in X^* is due to the sensitivity of harvesting costs to the stock level, i.e. the stock effect of $c'(X) < 0$. Note also that $p - c(X)$ is the marginal value of the population (i.e. the net value of a harvested unit), which is an increasing function of X.

If the price of ivory, p, varies with time, but the cost and discount rate remain constant, then (6) becomes:

$$F'(X) - \frac{c'(X)F(X)}{p - c(X)} = \delta - \frac{\dot{p}}{p - c(X)}, \tag{7}$$

where price changes imply that the value of the asset, X, is changing independently of its natural growth, and $\dot{p}/p - c(X)$ is simply the relative rate of growth of the marginal value of the asset.

If c(X) is constant, i.e. harvesting costs are independent of the population level, then (7) becomes:

$$F'(X) = \delta - \frac{\dot{p}}{p - c},$$
(8)

which implies that ivory price increases reduce the effective value of δ and therefore an increased optimal elephant stock level, X*. In other words, it is desirable to exploit the stock less heavily for ivory when prices are increasing, because it will be worthwhile to harvest at a later time.

It is easy to see that extinction of elephant populations will occur if p > c, and F''(X) < 0. For example, for large values of δ, (8) may have no solution; i.e., X* → as δ → ∞.

In the case of the logistic function (1), condition (8) becomes:

$$r(1 - 2X/K) = \delta - \frac{\dot{p}}{p - c},$$
(9)

which has no solution if the right hand side of (9) is greater than r, since r(1 - 2X/K) has a maximum value of r when X* = 0. Equation (9) therefore implies the following conditions:

1. X* > 0 (i.e. no extinction) if either p < c or
   δ - $\dot{p}$/(p - c) < r, and
2. X* = 0 (i.e. extinction occurs) if both p ≥ c and
   δ - $\dot{p}$/(p - c) > r.

Notes

1. Recent estimates from Ian Douglas-Hamilton of IUCN's African Elephant and Rhino Specialist Group, October 1989. Previous estimates from IUCN/WWF/UNEP, *Elephants and Rhinos in Africa – A Time for Decision*, (1982) based on findings and recommendations of the African Elephant and Rhino Specalist Group.
2. J. Beddington, R. Mace, M. Basson and E-J. Gulland, "The Impact of the Ivory Trade on the African Elephant Population". A report to the ITRG by RRAG, London (1989).
3. See Douglas-Hamilton, op. cit. (Note 1) and Beddington *et al.*, op. cit. (Note 2). Douglas-Hamilton, p. 5, notes that "until the equatorial forest is censured it will remain the last great mystery concerning elephant numbers and trends. It could turn out to have the greatest component of the African elephant population."

4. J.H. Poole, "The Effects of Poaching on the Age Structures and Social and Reproductive Patterns of Selected East African Elephant Populations". Final report to the African Wildlife Foundation, in the ITRG Report, *The Ivory Trade and the Future of the African Elephant*, prepared for the Second Meeting of the CITES African Elephant Working Group, Gabarone, Botswana, (July 1989).

5. Elephants are "K-selected" – see James Wilen, "Bioeconomics of Renewable Resource Use", in Allen Kneese and James Sweeney, *Handbook of Natural Resources and Energy Economics*, vol. 1 (North-Holland: Amsterdam, 1985.) The figure of 6 per cent is from Graeme Caughley, *A Projection of Ivory Production and its Implications for the Conservation of African Elephants*, CSIRO Consultancy Report to CITES (CSIRO: Australia, 1988). However, Poole, op. cit. (Note 4) argues that the growth rate is likely to be much lower for poached populations.

6. There are two compelling arguments. The first is that the welfare of future generations is a public good to the present generation and that, therefore, the present generation under-invests in future welfare, which is formally equivalent to saying that the discount rate is too high. The second argument is that the social treatment of uncertainty should be different from the private treatment of uncertainty. Society can pool risks across a large number of projects so that discount rate because of risk is less for society than for a private investor who cannot pool risks by "portfolio spreading". Additionally, society can pool risks across many different people (or at least the number of taxpayers) so that the risk premium to be attached to the underlying discount rate tends to zero. For further discussion of these arguments see D.W. Pearce, A. Markandya and E.B. Barbier, *Blueprint for a Green Economy* (Earthscan: London, 1989).

7. See G. Hardin, "The Competitive Exclusion Principle", *Science*, 131, (1960) pp. 1291–7, and I.S.C. Parker and A.D. Graham (1988), "Elephant Decline: An Hypothesis" and "Men, Elephants and Competition". Draft documents, Nairobi, Kenya.

8. T.M. Swanson, *International Regulation of the Ivory Trade*, LEEC Discussion Paper, 89–04 (LEEC: London, 1989).

9. R.B. Martin, *Establishment of African Ivory Export Quotas and Associated Control Procedures*, Report to the CITES Secretariat (Geneva, August 1985).

10. I. Douglas-Hamilton, (1988). "African Elephant Population Study", Phase 2 of African Elephant Database Project, executed by WWF in cooperation with Global Environment Monitoring System, for the Commission of the European Communities, UNEP.

11. UNDP and World Bank, *African Economic and Financial Data*, (World Bank: Washington DC, 1989), Table 1–27.

12. E. B. Barbier, "Sustaining Agriculture on Marginal Land: A Policy Framework", *Environment*, vol. 31, no. 9 (November 1989), pp. 12–17. Douglas Southgate, *The Economics of Land Degradation in the Third World*, Environment Department Working Paper no. 2 (World Bank: Washington DC, May 1988).

13. Stuart A. Marks, *The Imperial Lion: Human Dimensions of Wildlife Management in Central Africa*, (Westvies: Boulder, Colorado, 1983), p. 54; and Camilla Toulmin, *Economic Behaviour Among Livestock-Keeping Peoples: A Review of the Literature on the Economics of Pastoral Production in the Semi-Arid Zones of Africa*, Development Studies Occasional Paper no. 25, (University of East Anglia, May 1983).

14. World Resources Institute and the International Institute for Environment and Development, *World Resources 1988–89* (Basic Books: New York, 1989), Table 2.6.

15. Barbier, op. cit. (Note 12); Anil Markandya and David Pearce, "Natural Environments and the Social Rate of Discount", *Project Appraisal*, vol 3, no. 1 (March 1988), pp 2–12.

16. E.B. Barbier, *The Economic Value of Ecosystems: 1 – Tropical Wetlands*. LEEC Gatekeeper 89-02, (LEEC, 1989).

17. G. Brown and W. Henry, *The Economic Value of Elephants*, LEEC Discussion Paper 89-12, (LEEC, 1989).

18. D. Western, "The Ecological Value of Elephants: A Keystone Role in African Ecosystems", in the ITRG Report, *The Ivory Trade and the Future of the African Elephant* (See Note 4 for details.)

19. See Colin W. Clark, *Mathematical Bioeconomics: The Optimal Management of Renewable Resources* (John Wiley: New York, 1976).

2 AFRICAN EXPORTS: QUANTITY AND VALUE

Introduction

The previous chapter described the desperate plight of African elephant populations and the role of the ivory trade in precipitating their decline. The problem has clearly accelerated over the 1980s, and has led to the recent decision by CITES for an indefinite ban on the ivory trade.

This chapter focuses on the supply of ivory exports by Africa. Estimates of the *volume* of African ivory exports over the period 1950–88 are made. The *value* of Africa ivory exports is also calculated for the period 1979–88. Subsequent chapters discuss the role of demand and the international efforts to regulate the ivory trade.

Background to Africa's Ivory Trade

The African trade in elephant ivory has a long history, which has been well documented. Only the trends of the last 65 years will be discussed here, as these present the relevant background to the current trade situation.

1925–71: East Africa ivory trade

One of the important pre-war centres of the ivory trade was East Africa. Detailed colonial trade reports for Kenya, Uganda and Tanzania captured these trade flows. In his unique report on *The East African Elephant Ivory Trade, 1925–1970*, Parker made an extensive analysis of the East African ivory trade for the period from 1925 to 1971.[1] The total quantity of ivory imported, traded within or exported from these three countries amounted to just over 550 tonnes in 1925. The volume of trade increased to around 2,860 tonnes in the early 1960s, after which, following Congo's Independence and the Revolution in Tanzania, the volume of traded ivory declined dramatically to less than 1,100 tonnes in the late 1960s.

The total quantity of ivory exported from East Africa between

1925–69 inclusive was a minimum of 36,851 tonnes. At the end of 1969 there was a stock of approximately 23.1 tonnes held in East Africa. By combining the figure of stocks held at the end of 1969 and total exports during 1925–69, and using an estimated average ivory weight per elephant, it is possible to derive a very rough estimate of the number of elephants killed during this period to support the trade in ivory. Using average ivory weights of between 70–80 kg, approximately 500,000 to 600,000 elephants were harvested for their ivory in East Africa between 1925 and 1969. The price of ivory dropped from an initial high of 17 Kenya schillings per pound (Ksch/lb) in 1925 to 5 Ksch/lb in the early 1930s, and then gradually increased to over 20 Ksch/lb in 1965.

The UK was East Africa's largest ivory buyer between 1925 and 1929, accounting for nearly half of total exports. However, with the onset of World War II the UK's trading postion declined to less than 3 per cent of total exports, and never recovered its market share. During the latter half of the inter-war period India emerged as the major ivory buyer. Between 1940–44, India was responsible for over 80 per cent of total exports from East Africa. This position ended after Independence, when economic pressures led to restrictions on imports of luxury goods into India. After the war, Hong Kong emerged as the major buyer of East African ivory, importing over 50 per cent of the total volume of trade, with Japan accounting for approximately 15 per cent in the early 1960s.

1950–78: African ivory trade

The total volume of all African ivory exports increased rapidly after World War II. There also occurred important shifts in the centres of trade. As in the case of the East African trade, Hong Kong and Japan assumed major roles in the world ivory market, with Japan a dominant end-use consumer and Hong Kong an entrepôt trader in raw ivory (see Chapter 3). However, as a broad generalization, the ivory trading routes were still heavily influenced by recent colonial history. Anglophone Africa tended to ship to Anglophone entrepôts, using Germany as an important trading route but also shipping direct to Hong Kong, and Francophone countries shipped to Francophone entrepôts, predominantly Belgium, with the ivory usually going to East Asia. Over the 1950-78 period, Tanzania, Kenya, Uganda, Sudan and Zambia appeared to have major roles in this export trade.

Belgium, the UK, France and West Germany were the European countries with a significant role in the world ivory trade. Belgium was the major European entrepôt for ivory in the post-war period.[2] Between 1950 and 1978 Belgium handled large volumes of tusks as a trade commodity, but actually had very little internal consumption of raw ivory and never developed a carving or ivory working industry of any consequence. From the mid-1970s, "bonded" ivory was not included in Belgium's customs statistics, giving a false impression that Belgium's entrepôt role had declined whereas it actually continued to trade heavily in ivory. The UK, like Belgium, traditionally traded in raw ivory, with little – approximately 5 tonnes per annum – being consumed domestically.

Although the French African colonies (e.g. what are now the Central African Republic, Cameroon, Senegal, Ivory Coast) were prime ivory-producing lands, France never developed an ivory entrepôt trade similar to that of the UK or Belgium. However, France did develop a domestic carving industry, peaking in the early 1970s with imports in the region of 75–85 tonnes per annum, but declining to around 10 tonnes per annum thereafter. In contrast, West Germany was a major ivory-consuming nation during the 1950s to early 1970s (25–30 tonnes per annum), and abruptly after 1974 increased its imports to as much as 70 tonnes per annum. This was for its current internal consumption, establishing stocks for future use, and for its role as a re-exporting centre, with its market Hong Kong.

The USA had a minor role in the raw ivory trade until the late 1970s, importing less than 10 tonnes per annum on average. However, there has always been a strong demand for worked ivory imports as finished goods in the USA (see Chapter 3). Following the proposal of a ban on the importation of ivory, imports rose to as much as 35 tonnes in 1977 as the US domestic industry tried to pre-empt the ban and build ivory stocks.

During the period from 1950–78, India's economy was constrained by strict macro-economic policies, including heavy import duties imposed on luxury goods such as ivory. Official import statistics reflect a rapid decline of ivory imports from over 150 tonnes per annum in the early 1950s to less than 50 tonnes in the late 1960s. Following a brief, erratic increase to nearly 100 tonnes in 1971, imports fell again to less than 10 tonnes per annum in the late 1970s. However, it is possible that the official import statistics do not reflect the real imports of ivory into India, because high import taxes created a significant incentive to "hide" actual imports.

Thus the vast majority of African raw ivory exports between 1950 and 1978 were ultimately destined for East Asia, particularly Hong Kong and Japan. Hong Kong's role as the major ivory trader was established in the 1950s, importing around 100 tonnes per annum and growing to over 600 tonnes per annum in the early 1970s. In the late 1970s the growth of Hong Kong's demand slowed down, settling at around 500–600 tonnes per annum. Japan had for a long while been the second major trader in ivory after Hong Kong. However, Japan's imports continued to rise rapidly, from under 100 tonnes in the early 1950s to around 600 tonnes in the late 1970s. By then, Japan was threatening Hong Kong's dominant position as the world's major ivory trader, both in terms of domestic consumption and role as a redistributer of imported ivory. The following chapter provides a comprehensive analysis of the demand for ivory by Hong Kong and Japan, which is a crucial determinant of the world ivory trade.

The 1970s also saw the emergence of other key countries in the ivory trade. Prior to 1976, Singapore played an insignificant role, purchasing little from a variety of sources and exporting a similar amount. From 1976 onwards, Kenya began using Singapore as a routing point to Hong Kong and Japan, and thus imports and re-exports rose to over 30 tonnes per annum. More ominous was the use of other staging points, such as Dubai and the Arab Emirates, for illegal exports of ivory from Africa.

1976–89: the Appendix II era

The impact of the increased ivory trade on African elephants was evident in the post-war period. This led to a number of regulatory measures to manage elephant populations and to control the ivory trade. Since the early 1960s, most of the range states[3] have introduced either bans or strict regulations on elephant hunting and the trade in ivory. In addition, in 1976 CITES included the African elephant in Appendix II of the Convention. This meant that a CITES permit for trade in elephant products, including ivory, was required. Essentially, all ivory not carrying such a permit would be internationally recognized as illegal ivory, and Parties to the Convention should not trade in these products. Because of concern over further declines in elephant populations, in 1985 CITES parties introduced a Management Quota System (see p. 115), which was put into effect in 1986. This required each range state to submit a quota of elephant tusks, and all parties to trade only in ivory that is part of the quota system.

Estimating African Ivory Exports: 1950–88

To derive a measure of trends in African ivory exports since 1950 is a task fraught with difficulties. There are problems with African export data, and as discussed in Appendix 2.1, the methodology for combining data sets and eliminating double counting is fairly basic.

The trade statistics for ivory leaving Africa have always been very unreliable. Exporters have an incentive to conceal from the customs

Table 2.1: Overall African exports of unworked ivory compared to Parker's (1979) world trade estimates (in tonnes)

	Ex-Africa (LEEC est.)[a]	Parker "minimum world imports"[b]
1950	204	29
1951	318	87
1952	254	183
1953	295	266
1954	305	201
1955	313	212
1956	348	263
1957	329	243
1958	259	261
1959	380	334
1960	412	391
1961	282	235
1962	348	350
1963	319	288
1964	459	485
1965	403	440
1966	371	450
1967	468	537
1968	532	622
1969	620	648
1970	564	631
1971	488	493
1972	573	690
1973	878	1,236
1974	573	923
1975	598	923
1976	934	1,153
1977	738	993
1978	774/882[c]	993

Notes: [a] From D. Pearce and C. Pearce, "Aggregate African Ivory Exports 1950 to 1987", Economics Working Paper ITRG/EG 89–08, (LEEC, 1989).
[b] From I. Parker, *The Ivory Trade*, (US Fish and Wildlife Service: Washington DC, 1979).
[c] Lower figure from Pearce and Pearce, op. cit. Higher figure results from assuming all Hong Kong imports are derived from Africa and are not picked up in any other importing country statistics (e.g. Europe).

officials the real volume and value of the trade and so evade export duties. Any illegal or smuggled trade from Africa will obviously not be recorded in the export statistics. As a result, the trade data have consistently shown that the receiving countries import nearly twice as much as the African countries report as being exported. Because of this, it is preferable to use country-of-origin (COO) import statistics from the customs data of ivory-importing countries rather than to rely on African ivory export statistics.

Estimates of the volume of total African exports from 1950 to 1988 are given in Table 2.1, and in Table 1.2 of Chapter 1. As discussed in Appendix 2.1, the breakdown in the long-term trend between these two tables reflects changes in the way the ivory trade data have been computed. The only authoritative source on trade data up until 1979 is the Parker Report.[4] After 1979, the Wildlife Trade Monitoring Unit (WTMU) began compiling data as part of its efforts to monitor enforcement of the Appendix II CITES agreement. Figure 2.1 shows the trend in the total volume of African exports from 1950 to 1988.

Figure 2.1 indicates the long-run increasing trend in African ivory

---

Figure 2.1: African unworked ivory exports, 1950–88

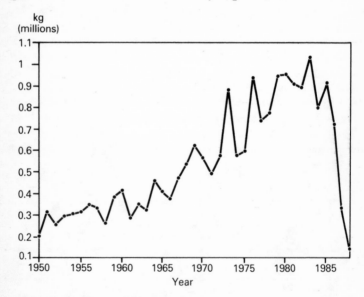

Source: London Environmental Economics Centre.

---

exports since 1950. In the 1950s, ivory exports averaged around 200–300 tonnes a year, rising to 300–400 tonnes in the 1960s. In the 1970s the trade was much more volatile, but it never fell much below 500 tonnes per annum, and reached a high of over 900 tonnes in 1976. Up until the mid-1980s, African ivory exports were running at around 800–900 tonnes annually, peaking at over 1,000 tonnes in 1983. But in recent years there has been a noticeable decline, with exports falling to below 350 tonnes in 1987.[5]

The crucial question is what has caused this recent decline? There are two opinions. On the one hand, the severe reduction of the African elephant population over the last decade may be a sufficient explanation. Quite simply, as explained in the previous chapter, the elephant has become a victim of "the economics of extinction". It has been hunted to such extreme limits that even the ivory trade itself has been undermined. On the other hand, the decline in the ivory trade also coincides with the implementation of the CITES quota system agreed in 1985. There are two possible reasons for this coincidence: the first is that the Management Quota System has been effective. There is certainly evidence that CITES-inspired legislation adopted by member states has been instrumental in exposing, and presumably halting, some illegal trade, as well improving the management of the legal trade.[6] But Chapter 5 explains why this is unlikely to be the case in general.

Another possible explanation is that the adoption of CITES restrictions has resulted in driving the trade "underground".[7] In the past it has been possible to chart the movement of the trade away from compliant states and toward the non-compliant by reference to customs statistics. That is, a state with no CITES legislation has no laws disallowing ivory trade, and thus there are no incentives for untruthful reporting to the customs authorities. In short, the cumulative impact of the widespread adoption of CITES legislation may have been the encouragement of the under-reporting of the ivory trade.

However, we will probably never know which of these has been the principal cause. Possibly both factors have been significant. As from 1990, the CITES ban will have the greatest effect on the pattern of African exports – whether it succeeds in halting the elephant's decline or not.

The Value of African Ivory Exports: 1979–88

The main African ivory exporters in recent years are listed in Table 1.2 of Chapter 1. The exporters are not necessarily the elephant-producing countries, however. Several African countries have acted

Table 2.2: Implicit raw ivory export prices, 1979-88 (US$/kg)

	1979	1980	1981	1982	1983	1984	1985	1986	1987	1988
Burundi	61	60	59	72	59	71	56	63	150	
Botswana	73	78	86	85	76	na	86	85	180	
CAR	76	71	77	84	65	64	92	116	143	
Congo	61	61	80	73	60	62	73	92	106	
Kenya	72	42	32	53	72	53	34	75	167	
Sudan	42	31	31	40	35	64	50	59	61	
Tanzania	71	65	55	65	37	58	78	48	37	
S. Africa	57	63	65	68	50	64	45	91	134	
Zimbabwe	na	na	na	na	54	69	73	80	174	
Zaire	83	70	48	59	51	47	41	100	77	
Unweighted Average	66.2	60.1	59.2	66.6	55.9	61.3	62.8	80.9	122.9	150*

Note: * For 1988 we assume a price of US$150/kg.
CAR refers to Central African Republic.
These are implicit import prices (customs, insurance and freight based).

as entrepôts for neighbouring states. These include Sudan, Burundi, the Central African Republic (CAR) and Congo, each of which exported more than 900 tonnes of ivory between 1979 and 1988. For many years, Burundi, located between Zaire and Tanzania, had just one elephant. In 1986 this elephant apparently produced 23,000 tonnes of ivory, all carefully documented as originating in the country! In South Africa, elephants were virtually wiped out at the turn of the century, but strictly enforced conservation measures have allowed the population to expand to a controlled 8,200 today. At maximum reproductive rates, the elephants could produce no more than 885 tusks per year. However South Africa set export quotas in recent years at 8,000, 10,000 and 12,000 tusks.

Table 2.2 shows one calculation of implict ivory prices. The methodology used for calculating prices over 1979–87 is discussed in Appendix 2.2. Figure 2.2 displays the resulting trend in average world ivory prices over the last decade. Up until 1985, ivory prices remained fairly stable at around $55/kg. However, in the late 1980s, prices shot up rapidly, to over $120/kg in 1987 and possibly $150/kg or more in 1988. This rise corresponds to the recent tailing-off in African exports. In other words, ivory appears to have been subject to a classic *excess demand*: as the supply of a particularly good quality of African ivory

Figure 2.2: Ivory prices, 1979–88

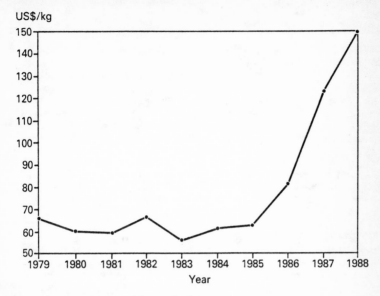

Source: London Environmental Economics Centre.

has diminished, the price has risen substantially as demand fails to be satisfied.

Preliminary indications are that ivory prices in 1989 will have fallen dramatically in response to the pressures on CITES to ban the ivory trade. It became increasingly clear in the summer of 1989 that the CITES meeting in October would probably result in a ban, and a number of key consumer countries such as the USA and members of the EEC pre-emptively announced their own unilateral bans. Japan initially imposed a ban on trade via Hong Kong, although later Japan imposed its own complete ban on the trade in elephant ivory. The result was that, even before the CITES decision in October 1989 to list the elephant on Appendix I, ivory prices were already falling as traders began quickly moving their stocks of both worked and raw ivory onto the market in anticipation of the ban, and as ivory trade routes to Asia were disrupted. For example, in September 1989, TRAFFIC – the World Wide Fund (WWF) for Nature's wildlife trade-monitoring network – reported that over the previous three months, costs of both raw and worked ivory in Hong Kong fell by

Table 2.3: Value of African ivory exports, 1979–88 (in US$)

	1979	1980	1981	1982	1983	1984
Angola	0	0	296	0	2,795	613
Benin	0	0	0	12,987	0	0
Botswana	840,674	330,189	518,000	312,287	311,922	223,622
Burkina	0	0	2,072	1,732	0	0
Burundi	9,193,856	7,556,553	3,611,733	3,091,306	6,950,606	11,278,526
Cameroon	485,312	472,987	129,944	174,026	48,577	116,225
CAR	11,997,625	10,977,866	6,344,109	13,432,887	11,395,327	7,453,590
Chad	1,788,525	252,420	796,595	1,837,760	1,886,234	268,678
Congo	6,167,060	10,547,490	14,017,613	6,791,069	2,990,594	5,842,013
I. Coast	46,406	64,788	64,528	979,886	31,248	21,516
Djibouti	0	0	0	0	0	0
Egypt	0	0	1,776	0	559	0
Ethiopia	0	0	0	0	0	10,544
Gabon	247,958	89,068	65,534	15,917	48,857	13,670
Ghana	33,100	1,683	4,736	7,459	839	1,839
Guinea	0	601	0	0	839	0
Kenya	3,025,539	1,814,900	334,006	825,773	224,271	789,728
Liberia	5,958	6,311	0	666	950	245
Malawi	37,072	120	43,512	17,516	66,577	20,168
Mali	0	0	0	0	0	0
Mozambique	393,824	42,911	592	57,942	894	58,848
Namibia	1,456,731	105,415	8,998	378,488	91,788	186,352
Niger	0	0	0	0	0	0
Nigeria	13,902	38,464	30,902	27,972	15,261	9,931
Rwanda	0	10,217	4,736	0	0	0
S. Africa	2,777,090	2,115,400	1,943,358	1,893,971	2,544,512	2,222,493
Senegal	0	16,407	5,269	0	56	368
S. Leone	0	2,885	1,717	666	280	0
Somalia	0	6,491	1,079,808	497,369	47,627	444,241
Sudan	8,237,796	12,358,123	15,899,877	18,536,711	18,856,020	4,162,822
Swaziland	0	0	0	0	0	0
Tanzania	2,203,335	2,702,276	1,582,890	1,166,499	864,438	2,747,711
Togo	0	12,020	1,184	0	2,795	9,808
Uganda	1,686,180	1,159,449	2,671,400	817,049	710,042	6,102,231
Zaire	10,608,351	5,072,380	2,679,155	5,214,713	8,780,996	5,529,199
Zambia	1,029,476	1,349,365	1,658,962	2,261,536	1,023,417	101,697
Zimbabwe	200,586	99,165	77,138	942,190	786,793	1,275,898
Min. Total	62,476,382	57,205,945	53,580,440	59,296,378	57,685,111	48,892,574
Maximum						
Burundi	9,591,056	11,405,958	3,639,498	3,091,306	7,385,732	11,278,526
Sudan	8,237,796	21,282,131	16,296,517	19,202,711	18,856,020	4,162,822
Max. Total	62,873,582	69,979,358	54,004,845	59,962,378	58,120,236	48,892,574

Note: CAR refers to Central African Republic.

	1985	1986	1987	1988	Total
Angola	0	0	0	0	3,704
Benin	628	0	0	0	13,615
Botswana	1,037,393	29,124	45,596	9,750	3,658,557
Burkina	1,256	0	0	0	5,060
Burundi	13,515,690	11,177,063	6,178,183	1,298,250	73,851,766
Cameroon	99,915	65,125	384,923	380,700	2,357,734
CAR	7,323,978	1,566,790	254,403	39,000	70,785,584
Chad	2,386	0	197,377	0	7,029,975
Congo	4,539,184	1,379,992	10,615,733	2,820,900	65,711,648
I. Coast	28,511	11,083	60,344	148,200	1,456,510
Djibouti	0	0	0	1,635,150	1,635,150
Egypt	188	405	0	0	2,928
Ethiopia	388,920	372,140	216,796	324,000	1,312,400
Gabon	23,362	38,913	517,655	2,031,300	3,092,261
Ghana	0	5,663	9,218	0	64,537
Guinea	314	0	0	0	1,754
Kenya	1,176,432	144,568	17,575	0	8,352,792
Liberia	1,570	1,699	3,195	0	20,594
Malawi	52,124	6,391	117,738	114,300	475,518
Mali	0	405	369	0	774
Mozambiqu	54,008	129,197	778,694	1,095,300	2,612,210
Namibia	115,364	102,581	123	0	2,445,840
Niger	0	0	2,212	0	2,212
Nigeria	14,570	7,443	0	900,000	1,058,445
Rwanda	281,658	260,822	0	0	557,433
S. Africa	3,111,426	3,311,642	2,178,157	1,133,550	23,231,599
Senegal	3,454	0	3,687	0	29,241
S. Leone	628	0	0	0	6,176
Somalia	283,102	5,211,012	592,255	0	8,161,905
Sudan	1,388,885	6,286,415	8,551,259	0	94,277,908
Swaziland	17,333	0	0	0	1,333
Tanzania	7,157,190	24,418,694	6,928,365	6,387,150	56,158,548
Togo	10,676	7,281	16,592	0	60,356
Uganda	12,598,968	251,114	492	42,150	26,399,075
Zaire	1,372,306	1,852,529	1,456,734	1,651,350	44,217,713
Zambia	907,711	892,974	531,543	243,300	9,999,981
Zimbabwe	1,433,347	642,831	994,630	1,047,450	7,500,028
Min. Total	57,302,488	58,173,896	40,653,845	21,301,800	516,568,864
Maximum					
Burundi	13,515,690	18,148,459	6,178,183	1,298,250	85,532,658
Sudan	1,388,885	6,286,415	8,551,259	0	104,264,556
Max. Total	57,302,488	65,145,291	40,653,845	21,301,800	538,236,404

Source: Derived from the volume of African raw ivory exports in Table 1.2, multiplied by the unweighted average implicit ivory export price in Table 2.2.

30–50 per cent, ivory stockpiles in Africa were not being purchased and the small quantities of ivory bought by local carving factories were going for half their former price.[8]

However, other indications are not so favourable. For example, in early 1990 there have been reports of increased poaching activity in Kenya.

One advantage of the quota system operating before the ban is that it produced a two-tier market, with legal ivory exports commanding much higher prices than illegal exports.[9] The imposition of the ban ends this two-price structure. Ivory prices will probably continue to be depressed, at least in the short term, in the wake of the ban, but this may only be a reduction of the previous high legal prices to the much lower illegal price levels (see Chapter 1, Table 1.2). What the long-term trend in ivory prices will be is essentially dependent on the effectiveness of the ban and the speed with which illegal ivory trading routes are established (see Chapter 6).

By taking the best estimates of ivory exports (see Table 1.2 in Chapter 1) and multiplying them by the representative implicit prices per kg of ivory from Table 2.2, the value of ivory exports to Africa in recent years can be determined. As shown in Table 2.3, the value of annual ivory exports recorded by importing countries, between 1979 to 1988 inclusive, averaged around $50–60 million for Africa as a whole. This figure only represents the value of raw ivory exports, and does not include ivory used in the domestic carving industry, or any revenue from hides and meat.

However, not all of this raw ivory export revenue actually goes to Africa. The values in Table 2.3 are obtained from the customs and CITES statistics of *importing* countries, and therefore are based on c.i.f. prices, that is, the prices include charges for customs, insurance and freight for the trade and probably overstate the actual export receipts to Africa by 10–15 per cent. In addition, as raw ivory is often shifted by traders from one destination to another before it reaches the final consuming nation (see Chapter 3), the import values of raw ivory include any marketing margins involved in the international trade. These margins probably overstate the actual receipts to Africa by another 10–15 per cent. Thus, a more realistic estimate of the total raw ivory export revenue received annually by African countries is $35–45 million.

Ivory export revenue of $35–45 million is a tiny fraction of annual African exports of all goods and services and suggests that Africa, as a whole, would suffer comparatively little loss from sacrificing some of these current revenues from ivory for sustainable management of the elephant population. Even the loss of a large share of this revenue to

Africa, which will be one result of the CITES ban, does not appear to be substantial.

However, the revenue is significant for a few individual countries. For example, in the Central African Republic, ivory exports up to 1985 were of fairly continuous significance with export values in the range of $10–25 million per annum. Those countries which dominate the export of ivory are also those where non-consumptive use values, such as tourism, have the lowest prospect, namely Congo, Sudan, Uganda and Zaire. These individual countries may thus have a substantial financial incentive to trade in elephant ivory. Countries with tourist trade, including Kenya, Zambia and Zimbabwe, tend to have low ivory export values. Zimbabwe's comparatively low export values for raw ivory are consistent with its use of indigenous culling to support a domestic carving industry. While harvested ivory is not of great value as an export to most African nations, with the possible exception of the Central African Republic, there is no implication that African countries should not be compensated for lost revenues. As Chapters 5 and 6 show, it is of fundamental importance to provide incentives to the exporting nations to desist from trade.

Intra-Africa Trade and the African Carving Industry

So far we have only discussed exports of ivory from Africa to the rest of the world. However, ivory is also subject to a considerable amount of trading between African countries. Often this intra-Africa trade involves the transformation of ivory from "raw" tusks or pieces to worked or semi-worked ivory. This applies to raw ivory obtained by both legal or illegal means. For example, any raw legally or illegally produced ivory in an African country can follow a number of paths:

  i)   some of it may be retained in the country's stock;
 ii)   some may be processed into worked ivory;
iii)   some may be exported outside of Africa; and
 iv)   some may be exported to other African countries.

The worked ivory produced may follow a similar path:

  i)   some of it may be retained in the country's stock;
 ii)   some may be purchased by residents and remain within the country;
iii)   some may be exported as bulk commercial exports outside of Africa or to a third-party African country as an intermediate export stage; and
 iv)   some may be exported outside of Africa as tourist souvenirs or personal possessions.

Thus there is both a lively intra-Africa trade in ivory that is part of the process of exportation to the rest of the world, and there is a considerable African carving industry that has developed as part of this process. Moreover, the intra-Africa trade is both extremely elaborate and difficult to trace. Often it revolves around trade routes that facilitate the transformation of illegally acquired ivory from one African country into "legal" exports of worked and raw ivory from another country. This is one unfortunate consequence of a two-price structure for ivory: the large gap between legal and illegal prices provides an incentive to exploit any loophole for converting illegal to legal ivory. For example, in Southern African countries the quantities of legally worked ivory appear to be relatively small. Few countries produce even 3 tonnes and most produce much less. Yet customs data for Southern African countries suggest that more substantial amounts of worked ivory are traded. Loopholes are being exploited in the definition of worked ivory to take advantage of the laxer controls on this commodity. Pseudo-worked ivory (i.e. semi-worked ivory often with minimal carving or working and often only scratching) of large, cut pieces and polished tusks – often originating from illegally obtained raw ivory – are thus passed by customs officials in Southern Africa, traded in the region and eventually exported.[10]

Table 2.4 indicates an estimate of the intra-regional trade in ivory for Southern Africa, including trade between this region and other African countries. In 1988 this trade amounted to about 84 tonnes, of which 56 tonnes was raw ivory. The latter represents about 40 per cent of the actual volume of raw ivory exported from all of Africa in that year (see Chapter 1, Table 1.2). This suggests that a substantial amount of intra-African trading takes place before ivory leaves the continent.

Table 2.4 also shows that much intra-African trade, at least in the Southern African region, involves a substantial amount of illegally acquired raw ivory and movements of pseudo-worked ivory. Exports of illegal raw ivory within the region in 1988 amounted to 53 tonnes, or nearly 95 per cent of the total intra-regional trade in raw ivory. Pseudo-worked ivory amounted in total to 24 tonnes, of which 10 tonnes was illegal. However, the 14 tonnes of "legal" pseudo-worked ivory was invariably exported under the "worked ivory" category. Thus out of the total 15 tonnes of legal worked ivory exports, only 1 tonne (7 per cent) was probably bonafide legally worked ivory. As a rough indicator, the total regional trade of raw and pseudo-worked ivory of 80 tonnes represents about 9,000 elephants.

South Africa is clearly the focal point for the intra-regional trade, accounting for almost half of all imports. Botswana is significantly

Table 2.4: Intra-regional ivory trade in Southern Africa, 1988

Imports (tonnes)

	Angola	Botswana	Malawi	Mozamb.	S. Africa	Zambia	Zimbabwe	Others	Total RI	Total RL	Total PI	Total PL	Total WI	Total WL	Total Exports
Angola					12 RI			12 RI	24						24
Botswana					3 RI 10 PI 1 WL	1 RI			4		10			1	4 10 1
Malawi				1 RI					1						1
Mozamb.						1 RI		1 RI	2						2
S. Africa						1 RI			1						1
Zambia		2 RI 4 PL			1 RI			6 RI	9			4			9 4
Zimbabwe				1 RI	3 RL 3 WI	1 RI			2	3			3		2 3 3
Others		3 RI 10 PL		2 RI	5 RI				10			10			10 10
Total	0	19	0	4	38	4	0	19	53	3	10	14	3	1	84

Notes:
RI = Raw Ivory, Illegal WI = Worked Ivory, Illegal PI = Pseudo-Worked Ivory, Illegal
RL = Raw Ivory, Legal WL = Worked Ivory, Legal PL = Pseudo-Worked Ivory, Legal
Others = Other African Countries

Source: Calculated from date in R.B. Martin, "The Ivory Trade in Southern Africa", Report to I.S.C. Parker for the CITES Secretariat, Department of National Parks and Wildlife Management, Harare, Zimbabwe (1989).

involved in importing ivory from both inside and outside the region. Since 1987 Botswana has served as an important transit route into South Africa for illegal worked ivory which originated in Zambia, Zaire, Zimbabwe and possibly other countries. The scale of this transit route was probably larger in previous years. The tightening up of South Africa's CITES regulations after 1986 has made it very difficult for raw ivory from this route to get an export permit.[11] Angola and Zambia are also major exporters within Southern Africa. Nearly one quarter of the ivory appears to be imported into the region from other African countries.

Africa's carving industry is important to the intra-African ivory trade. This industry also generates its own, separate exports of tourist curios and personal items from ivory, such as carvings, sculptures, chess sets, jewellery and so forth. An extensive study of the carving

Table 2.5: The carving industry in selected Southern African countries

	Ivory consumed annually (tonnes)	Number of workers employed (approx.)	Annual value of sales (US$)	Avg. price (US$/kg)	Mark-up over raw ivory (%)
Zimbabwe (1983)	14–15 (2 RI)	182	8,000,000	552	720
South Africa (1983)	6 (1-2 RI)	80	2,000,000	312	400
Zambia (1985)	4–5 (0.5-1 RI)	10–15	370,000	82	450
Botswana (1982)	3 (? RI)	30	–	–	–
Malawi	2.25	90	275,000	120	400a/

Notes: a/ Assumes same mark-up as South Africa, which has a similar mark-up differential between wholesale and retail prices.
RI = illegal raw ivory estimates.

Sources: Based on data derived from E.B. Martin, "Zimbabwe's Ivory Carving Industry", *Traffic Bulletin* vol. 6, no. 2, (1984), pp. 33–8; E.B. Martin, "South Africa's Ivory Carving Industry", *Traffic Bulletin*, vol. 7., no. 1, (1985), pp. 12–15; E.B. Martin, "The Ivory Carving Industry of Zambia", *Pachyderm*, no. 7, (1986), pp. 12–15; E.B. Martin, "The Ivory Industry in Botswana", *African Elephant and Rhino Group Newsletter*, no. 3, (1984), pp. 5–7; E.B. Martin, "Malawi's Ivory Carving Industry", *Pachyderm*, no. 5, (1985), pp. 6–11.

industries in Southern Africa has been conducted by Esmond Martin, the results of which are shown in Table 2.5. At its height in the early 1980s, the region's industries consumed approximately 30 tonnes of ivory annually, employing around 400 or more workers full and part time, and generated sales revenues of at least $11 million a year.

With the exception of Malawi, which has a long-established carving industry owned and run by Africans, most Southern African carving industries sprang up in the 1970s and are operated by non-Africans – both whites and Asians.[12] This reflects not only the role of South Africa as the major trading focus for the Southern African industries but also the traditional role of Asians as entrepreneurs in most Southern African commercial ventures.

The $11 million in worked ivory revenues – from only five countries – were approximately one-fifth of the value of all African raw ivory exports over the same period (see Table 2.3). With the exception of Zimbabwe, where a large percentage (65 per cent) of purchases were by citizens and foreign residents for investment purposes or to circumvent foreign exchange controls, most of the output of the Southern African carving industry is bought by foreign tourists.[13] This suggests that tourist exports from the Southern African carving industry generated no less than $6 million a year.

A significant amount of illegal raw ivory – at least 7 tonnes – may have been used by the Southern African carving industries in the early 1980s (see Table 2.5). However, the proportion used varies significantly by country. At one extreme, Malawi may have been relying on illegal supplies for around 70 per cent of its raw carving ivory, whereas perhaps as little as 10 per cent accounted for Zimbabwe's carving supplies. The extremely high mark-up of average retail prices of worked ivory over the value of (legally acquired) raw ivory supplies was probably the major incentive to use illegal raw ivory in carving industries. By obtaining the much cheaper illegal supplies, a carving industry could substantially boost the mark-ups shown in the table.

The most up-to-date information on the Southern African carving industries is provided by Rowan Martin.[14] His findings suggest that the volume of ivory consumed by the industries was much lower in the late as opposed to the early 1980s. For example, in 1988 the total amount of raw ivory in Botswana turned into carvings was unlikely to have exceeded 2 tonnes, as Botswana has instead turned to importing legal and illegal worked ivory products, most likely from Zimbabwe. Yet in Zimbabwe, during the last few years, raw ivory consumption by its carving industry has fallen from 15 to 8 tonnes annually. Large amounts of Zimbabwean worked ivory – nearly 2 to 3 tonnes – are still being exported to South Africa by Zimbabweans to avoid foreign exchange controls. The South Africans in turn blame the influx of Zimbabwean carvings for the recent decline of their own industry, which has seen its annual ivory consumption fall from 6 tonnes to 1 tonne by the late 1980s. Sales of this ivory in South Africa are probably divided equally between direct tourist sales and exported commercial shipments. Similarly, in Zambia the raw ivory used annually for carving may be at most 1–1.5 tonnes, if the amount of illegal raw ivory used is still 0.5–1 tonnes. Only the Malawian carving industry may still be consuming raw ivory (both legally and illegally acquired) at the same rate throughout the 1980s.

Thus the total raw ivory consumed by the Southern African carving industries in the late 1980s must be less than 15 tonnes, half of what it was in the early 1980s. As the ivory carving industry has always been closely tied to the fortunes of the continent's total ivory trade – beginning with the ivory trade boom of the 1970s and peaking at the same time as the export trade in the early 1980s – the industry's recent decline must also be linked to the recent tailing off of ivory exports from Africa. The reasons for the apparent decline might therefore be the same for both: the decimation of Africa's elephant populations has meant that far less ivory is available, and the establishment of the CITES quota system in the late 1980s may have led to under-reporting of the actual exports of raw ivory. That is, more ivory is being traded illegally, i.e. as non-CITES ivory, and therefore escapes customs documentation as well. Most likely, the dramatic falls in elephant numbers, as indicated in the previous chapter, may have been the major factor. But it must be kept in mind that in most Southern African countries, elephant populations have been either stabilized or even increasing.

There might also be another factor to the decline of ivory exports in the late 1980s. Better enforcement of CITES regulations, public awareness campaigns and changing consumer tastes may have interacted with the decline in the quantity and quality of African ivory to change trade patterns and demand by the importing countries. It is to this issue of trade flows and demand that we now turn in the following chapter.

Appendix 2.1: An Approach to Estimating African Ivory Exports, 1950–88

This chapter provides an estimate of African ivory exports between 1950-88, which is summarized in Tables 2.1 and 1.2. The data can be used to construct a continuous series of data from 1950 to 1988 (see

Figure 2.1). However, it must be noted that there is a change in the way in which the series of ivory trade data has been computed between 1950 to 1988. Data up until 1979 is based on statistics from the Parker Report,[15] and after that date from data compiled by the Wildlife Trade Monitoring Unit (WTMU) in Cambridge. Thus, Table 2.1 shows the estimates for African ivory exports for 1950–78, whereas Table 1.2 displays the later estimates for 1979–88. The basic difference in the two sets of data arises from the treatment of country-of-origin (COO) import statistics, and the sources of the data.

To arrive at a combined data set for the entire 1950-88 period requires eliminating the problem of double counting in the more recent data sets provided by WTMU and in the historical data set in the Parker Report. The methodology applied to the WTMU data involves tracing trade flows recorded in one data set (the customs statistics) with the aid of another data set (CITES permits) to differentiate between an importer's assigned COO to a shipment of ivory compared to its last port of call (the country of export – COE).[16] It is not possible to apply a similar analysis to the longer run historical data in the Parker Report, simply because CITES was not in existence. This means that the best estimates of African exports in Table 1.2 are based on CITES and customs data, whereas the estimates in Table 2.1 are based on customs statistics only. Thus, the continuous series of data 1950–88 is likely to indicate the discontinuity in the method of collection, and perhaps the data collected.

Further adjustments were also required for Parker's data for the ivory trade from 1950 to 1978. For example, Parker provides an overall estimate of minimum world imports as an indicator of trade activity. Given that the records for data are incomplete, he uses a mixture of East African customs export data and Hong Kong and Japan customs import statistics to obtain a best guess of the African ivory exports. It must be noted that the aggregate figures of minimum world trade of unworked ivory derived by Parker are *not* equivalent to African exports of ivory. Parker was not attempting to construct this indicator, but instead an indicator of the volume of trade.

To estimate the volume of ivory trade, Parker added, for example, Japan's total imports of ivory to Hong Kong's total imports of ivory. This is an acceptable procedure to determine trade activity. However, to compile the statistics for quantity of African exports, it is necessary to net out any double counting, for example of re-exports. The approach that we have taken to adjust Parker's figures is as follows.

In Japan, imports from Hong Kong, say, are recorded as having come from their country of origin rather than from Hong Kong.

Hong Kong will also record the same imports when it receives them from Africa before re-exporting them to Japan. Thus, the ivory imports will be recorded as being imported by both Japan and Hong Kong and will result in double counting. To get Japan's effective imports we simply need to deduct Hong Kong's exports to Japan. This adjustment is not significant until the early 1970s when such trade amounted to 20–60 tonnes annually, becoming very significant in the later 1970s when it grew to 100-200 tonnes annually. From Japan's effective imports we then deduct all non-African sources of Japan's imports.

A problem arises in Belgium with respect to bonded trade. For example, say an export goes from Africa to Belgium, where it is held in bond there before it goes to Hong Kong. Hong Kong records it as coming from Belgium, but Belgium does not record it as an import at all. The difficulty is that there is no apparent way of gauging the extent of bonded trade. There are two alternative procedures. One is to add up Hong Kong imports regardless of where they come from, and then ignore Belgium data. Alternatively, one can account only for Hong Kong imports stated as coming from Africa, then add recorded Belgium imports from Africa, and finally, add an estimate of Belgium bonded imports. The approach adopted here is to derive a "guesstimate" of Belgium's bonded trade imports by looking at Japanese and Hong Kong imports from Belgium.

Table 2.1 indicates our estimate of African ivory exports from 1950–78 and compares them to Parker's original calculations of minimum world exports.

Appendix 2.2: Estimating the Value of African Ivory Exports, 1979–88

Table 2.2 records prices for ivory from 1979 to 1988 by selected African countries. They are implicit import prices (c.i.f. based), as they are derived from the customs data for the importing countries. The prices are calculated by dividing local currency estimates of values by imported quantities, and then converting at the prevailing rate of exchange to a common dollar-of-the-day figure. The average implicit prices in Table 2.2 are unweighted values, determined through a two-stage process. For example, Kenya's exports to countries A, B, C are recorded by the importing nations A, B, C. Individual import values are aggregated across A, B, C, as are quantities. The two sums of value and quantity are then divided to give the average price shown here.

The databases are the WTMU value matrices and quantity

matrices for customs only. Because insufficient statistics were available to extend the value matrices to 1988, only an approximate estimate of average implicit ivory prices for this year is possible. Thus in Table 2.2 we assume a price of $150/kg for 1988. In some years Singapore has been excluded, as apparent inaccuracies in the figures result in extremely high unit values for ivory which could not realistically be correct.

Notes

1. I.S.C. Parker, *The East African Elephant Ivory Trade, 1925–1970*, a Wildlife Services Ltd Report to Botswana Game Industries (Pty) Ltd, (Francistown: Botswana, 1971). This pioneering report was the first study that examined overseas trade records as an indication of the extent of the ivory trade.
2. I.S.C. Parker, *The Ivory Trade*, (US Fish and Wildlife Service: Washington DC, 1979).
3. The term "range state" is often used, especially in CITES documentation, to refer to an African country countaining elephant populations.
4. Parker, op. cit. (Note 2).
5. Although 1988 statistics show a further decline to under 150 tonnes per annum, the data are too provisional to draw any conclusion about trends.
6. UNEP/GEMS, *The African Elephant*, UNEP/GEMS Environment Library, no. 3, (UNEP: Nairobi, 1989), pp. 34–6.
7. I.S.C. Parker report to the CITES Secretariat (1990).
8. "Ivory Prices Drop in Africa", *WWF News*, no. 61, (September/October 1989).
9. UNEP/GEMS, op.cit. p. 36 (Note 6). One encouraging result of the two-price structure is that it would make illegal poaching and trading appear less attractive as opposed to abiding by the rule of the legal trade. Unfortunately, the incentive to transform illegally acquired ivory into "legally sanctioned" exports of raw worked or pseudo-worked ivory is also increased (see section on "Intra-African Trade and the African Carving Industry" p. 39).
10. R.B. Martin, (1989), *The Ivory Trade in Southern Africa*, Report to I.S.C. Parker for the CITES Secretariat, Department of National Parks and Wildlife Management, Harare, Zimbabwe.
11. Martin, op.cit. (Note 10).
12. E.B. Martin, "Malawi's Ivory Carving Industry", *Pachyderm*, no. 5, (1989), pp. 6–11.
13. E.B. Martin, "Zimbabwe's Ivory Carving Industry", *Traffic Bulletin*, vol. 6, no. 2, (1984), pp. 33-8.

14. Martin, op.cit. (Note 10).
15. Parker, op.cit. (Note 2).
16. R. Luxmoore, J. Caldwell and L. Hithersay, "Comparison of CITES and Customs Statistics on the International Trade in Raw Ivory", Report to the Ivory Trade Review Group (1989).

3 THE IVORY TRADE FLOW: WORKED AND UNWORKED

Intermediate and Final Demand

In the previous chapter we discussed exports of ivory from Africa, as well as the critical role of intra-Africa trade. Although accounting for the exports of raw ivory is not easy, it is not nearly as difficult as tracing the exports of worked ivory as these may range from bulk shipment to individual tourist purchases and can cover such diverse commodities as jewellery, carvings, chess sets, furniture inlays, parts of musical instruments and so on. Thus no consistent statistics on worked ivory exports from Africa are available, although we were at least able to provide some idea of the elaborate links between the raw and worked ivory trade for Southern Africa.

This chapter examines the trade in ivory once it leaves Africa. As in the case of the intra-African trade, these international trade flows involve complex movements of both legal and illegal raw, worked and pseudo-worked ivory, as well as transformations of raw into various states of worked ivory. But as we are now dealing with global movements and transformations, the trade flows become even more difficult to trace. Important trading countries, such as Belgium and Hong Kong, have had long-standing involvement in the international ivory trade as entrepôts or middlemen in the flow of raw and worked ivory. The international carving industry may also be extremely fluid, moving from country to country as trading patterns, and possibly the regulations governing the trade, change.

Figures 3.1 and 3.2 give some idea of the global nature and complexity of the international ivory trade. The principal ivory-trading network channels African ivory exports to Asia, where ivory has long been a prize commodity, especially in Japan (Figure 3.1). There, ivory has traditionally been used for highly valued personal seals, ceremonial items, jewellery and carvings. In recent years, a major trading stage on the way to Asia has been Dubai, particularly for transforming illegal raw ivory into legal raw and worked exports. Hong Kong, as noted, is the principal entrepôt of the region and also has a substantial carving industry; however, Macau, Singapore and

Figure 3.1: Principal ivory trade flows: Africa to Asia

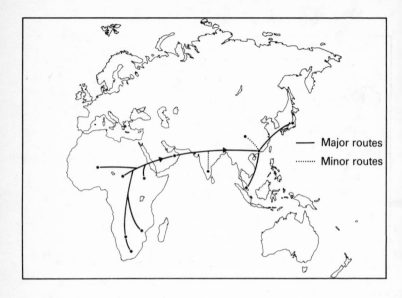

Source: London Environmental Economics Centre.

Taiwan have also become increasingly important staging centres for the trade. India has also periodically been a major ivory importer, and China may be increasing its demand.

However, linked to these principal trading routes is an even larger and more elaborate global trading network. One important chain in this network is shown in Figure 3.2. In the past, exports from Africa have also been shipped to its ex-colonial European powers. Belgium in particular, but also Germany, France and the UK may have been linked into this trade, which not only brings ivory into the European Economic Community (EEC) but may be additionally linked to Hong Kong and thus the Japanese and wider Asian markets. Much of the worked ivory produced in Hong Kong has traditionally been exported to North America, principally the USA.

The following sections will describe in more detail the difficulties involved in tracing ivory trade patterns and the international trade

Figure 3.2: Secondary ivory trade flows: the global network

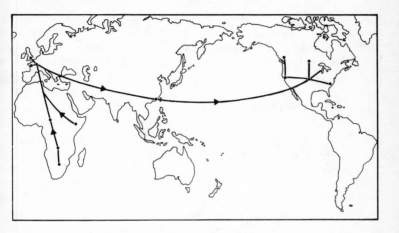

Source: London Environmental Economics Centre.

flows in worked and raw ivory. The role of the major importing countries involved in the intermediate and final demand for ivory will also be briefly discussed. A more extensive analysis of the demand for ivory by Hong Kong and Japan – the principal actors in the international ivory trade – will be presented in the next chapter.

Difficulties in Tracing Ivory Trade Flows

It is important to consider all available data sources to derive an estimate of the total volume of raw ivory entering into international trade from various centres in Africa. Simply looking at the export figures in the exporting countries' customs statistics, where they exist, does not give a reliable estimate of the total volume of ivory. Because of the illegal nature of the ivory trade as it leaves Africa, much of the ivory only appears in the official trade statistics after it has passed through one or more intermediate countries. At this stage it may pick up official documentation from CITES. However, CITES has only accounted for around 20 per cent of the recorded trade in recent years. Using these data, but primarily looking at importing country trade statistics, where there is less of an incentive to mislead and data figures are more realistic, export totals of raw ivory exports from Africa have been reconstructed (see Table 2.1).

The complexities of the trade in elephant ivory become even more apparent when the transition of raw to worked ivory and the trade flows of worked ivory are considered. Monitoring this trade is fraught with difficulties. Although import and export statistics for worked ivory derived from customs data covering the period from 1978–87 inclusive have been collected and compiled, this data is often even more unreliable and incomplete than in the case of raw ivory (see Appendix 3.1).[1] There is no one consistent unit for categorizing worked ivory. Individual countries use different categories, use a number of categories, and frequently change their categorization. The import/export data for worked ivory that is available is recorded with details of weight or value, or both.

The ivory may be worked to various degrees with no indication whether this is simple scratching, i.e. pseudo-worked, or intricate carving, e.g. ivory worked, ivory manufactured as artware, ivory adornments such as rings, bracelets, necklaces and so on. The categorization may also include a range of "other" articles, with no indication of what percentage is ivory: e.g. articles of horn, hair, hoof, whalebone, ivory, quill, shell or sponge. What is more, ivory may not be accounted for in the customs statistics if it is part of an object, for example, ivory piano keys may not be listed, as a piano comes under musical instruments with no reference to the ivory that it contains. (Again, see Appendix 3.1.)

Although the statistics of worked ivory data are plagued with difficulties they do give us some indication of the patterns of international flows of worked ivory. Monitoring the trade in worked ivory alongside raw ivory has also revealed shifts in trade between the two. One of the characteristics of the illegal ivory trade is its remarkable fluidity. Whenever one channel through which ivory is passing has been blocked, another has opened up almost immediately. Over recent years ivory has often passed through a number of staging points, such as Dubai, Singapore, Macao and Taiwan, each of which was chosen for the convenience of some legislative loophole.

Legal restrictions on ivory imports into Hong Kong have been easily exploited in the past. Although Hong Kong implemented import controls on raw ivory imports in 1986, no such restrictions on imports of worked ivory were put into effect until August 1988. Ivory traders from Hong Kong devised methods to avoid these controls on raw ivory by shifting trade to worked, and most often pseudo-worked, ivory. In one case, 67 carvers and 150 labourers were sent from Hong Kong to Dubai in the United Arab Emirates, to set up two carving factories. The traders were there able to buy poached ivory at a reduced price from established ivory traders and then carve the ivory sufficiently to pass as worked ivory. This semi-worked ivory could then be imported legally into Hong Kong and sold at a much higher value.[2] It is apparent that, due to the close interaction between raw and worked ivory, it is very difficult to monitor or control the trade in one without taking the other into consideration.

In the rest of this chapter we will discuss the roles of the major ivory trading countries and the stages of transition between raw ivory exports and worked ivory consumption. In particular, we discuss the remarkable fluidity of the shifts in the patterns of trading between countries and the relocation of carving centres. A further characteristic of the ivory trade is that there exists an intricate structure of the major ivory dealers who dominate the industry. Some consideration of this market organization sheds further light on the pattern of international trade in elephant ivory.

Trade Flows and Final Demand: Hong Kong and Japan

Together Hong Kong and Japan accounted for approximately 75 per cent of the total world imports, and 60 per cent of net imports, between 1979 and 1988 (see Chapter 1, Tables 1.2 and 1.3, and Chapter 4). In the early 1980s this amounted to around 500–600 tonnes of net raw ivory imports annually, whilst in the latter half of the 1980s this declined to around 150 tonnes of annual net imports of raw ivory. The trading patterns of the Hong Kong and Japan raw ivory trade will be discussed briefly below, but further analysis of this trade will be given in the following chapter.

Hong Kong
More ivory passes through Hong Kong than any other country. Hong Kong is the major ivory trader and has connections with the African suppliers of raw ivory and both the raw and worked ivory-consuming countries. Although it is the major processor of ivory, it consumes relatively little of the finished product. Hong Kong is heavily dependent upon the international market, especially the USA and the EEC, for the sale of its worked ivory products.

Of the sum total of between 7,625 and 7,955 tonnes of ivory exported from Africa between 1979 and 1988 (see Table 1.2 and Figure 4.6), 3,971 tonnes – that is, nearly 55 per cent – have been imported into Hong Kong.[3] Up until 1986, average imports of raw ivory into Hong Kong exceeded 500 tonnes annually. Since the CITES export quota system was implemented in 1986, levels of raw ivory imports have more than halved to an average of 225 tonnes annually.

Raw ivory imports into Hong Kong have followed a diverse range of trading routes. Direct trade links with Africa were developed in the early twentieth century, especially with the countries facing the Indian Ocean, such as Kenya, Sudan and Tanzania. Later trading links were also set up throughout Francophone Africa. In recent years, Hong Kong traders have attempted to establish direct links with Zaire, Congo and the Central African Republic. However, since 1979 only 30 per cent of raw ivory imports have come directly from African producing countries, with exports from Sudan and South Africa contributing a significant share. The majority of imports into Hong Kong are re-exports from other, intermediary, trading nations.

One of the major staging routes of raw ivory on its way to Hong Kong has been Belgium. According to custom statistics, over the past ten years from 1979–88 inclusive, Belgium has accounted for at least 25 per cent of all imports of raw ivory into Hong Kong. The recent tightening of Belgium's ivory import and export policies after joining CITES in 1984 has had some effect on this dominant position. Other European re-exporters, notably France and the UK, have also played significant roles in Hong Kong's raw ivory import trade.

A further 24 per cent of the total of raw ivory entering Hong Kong during the period 1979–88 has come from Japan. However, the tightening of Japan's trade controls as from 1986 reduced re-exports. Large quantities of ivory were imported into Hong Kong from the stockpiles in Singapore: 52,430kg in 1987 and 112,767kg in 1988. The imports of raw ivory stocks from Singapore detracted from the impact of the decreasing availability of raw ivory from Hong Kong's traditional trading partners.

Over 30 per cent, approximately 1,250 tonnes, of Hong Kong's gross raw ivory imports between 1979 to 1988 were later re-exported. The major importers of this raw ivory were Japan, China, India, Taiwan and Thailand. Japan, in particular, consumes over 60 per cent of these re-exports. Japan and Hong Kong have developed a special relationship in raw ivory transactions. Hong Kong imports large shipments containing ivory tusks and pieces in a variety of qualities and sizes. Hong Kong is able to sort this ivory, and then exports the larger, better quality tusks to Japan, which has a preference for this type of ivory for its carving industry. Ivory imports into Japan have consistently had a mean tusk weight of over 10 kg. Hong Kong carvers are willing to retain the smaller, lower valued

Table 3.1: Average market prices paid for ivory in Japan and Hong Kong (US$ kg)

	Japan	Hong Kong
1979	87	56
1980	84	55
1981	83	41
1982	82	41
1983	67	39
1984	75	49
1985	99	56
1986	227	61
1987	184	74

Source: E.B. Barbier, "The Demand for Unworked Ivory: A Case Study of Hong Kong", Economics Working Paper ITRG, 89–09 (April 1989) and E.B. Barbier, "The Demand for Unworked Ivory: A Case Study of Japan", Economics Working Paper ITRG, 89–01 (February 1989).

ivory pieces for their own carving industry; in Hong Kong the mean tusk weight has fallen from 8 kg to 4 kg over the course of the decade. The difference in the prices paid for ivory in Hong Kong and Japan is shown in Table 3.1.

Hong Kong regularly stores substantial quantities of ivory – as much as 670 tonnes of raw ivory were stockpiled in Hong Kong in early 1990. Hong Kong maintains its stocks of ivory for a variety of reasons. As international controls have become increasingly stricter, and the availability of raw ivory increasingly scarce, there has been a tendency for Hong Kong to buy up any ivory that is for sale and to store it for future use. This has meant that it has secured a regular supply of ivory for any in-house manufacturing requirements, as well as to meet local and foreign demand for supplies of raw ivory. Hong Kong may also store ivory as an "investment". Chapter 4 looks in greater detail at the incentives for storing ivory, especially as an investment and store of wealth.

The majority of raw ivory entering Hong Kong is consumed within Hong Kong's own carving industry, the remainder stockpiled or re-exported. Hong Kong is the largest worked-ivory producing country and during the last decade, from 1978-88 inclusive, Hong Kong has retained over 3,127 tonnes of net imports of raw ivory (see Table 4.4). Ivory carvings within Hong Kong are made up of:

    i)   sculptures and netsuke (30–40 per cent);
    ii) jewellery (20 per cent); and,
    iii) seals (recently a substantial 40–50 per cent).

Although Hong Kong has a dominant role in both raw ivory transactions and worked ivory processing, it actually consumes relatively little of the final goods within its country. Domestic consumption accounts for a mere 5 per cent of the total production of worked ivory in Hong Kong. Thus 95 per cent of Hong Kong's worked ivory is exported: 70–75 per cent directly through exports, 20–25 per cent indirectly through tourists purchasing ivory within Hong Kong.

Hong Kong exports worked ivory to a diverse range of countries all over the world. Between the period from 1979 to 1988, the total value of worked ivory exports from Hong Kong amounted to some $350 million, 35 per cent of which were destined for the USA, 29 per cent for the EEC (France alone 14 per cent, followed by Italy, Germany and Spain), 27 per cent for Japan, and 2 per cent for Singapore. Hong Kong also exports worked ivory to Africa. Between 1979 and 1988 Hong Kong exported approximately $4,000,000 worth of worked ivory to Africa, mainly to South Africa, Macao, Djibouti, Morocco and Botswana. Although this is only around 1 per cent of the total value of worked ivory exports from Hong Kong, the value is significant in terms of costs to Africa. This is especially clear when the imports of worked ivory from Africa are compared to the value of the raw ivory exports from Africa during the same period. That is, imports of $4 million from worked ivory from Hong Kong compared to exports of around $35–45 million from exports of raw ivory from Africa.

Estimates of the value added from carving raw ivory within Hong Kong are given in Table 3.2. These figures are derived by first of all calculating the total value of both worked ivory exports and worked ivory re-exports from Hong Kong. Second, from this sum export value, the value of raw ivory imports and any worked ivory imports are deducted. This final figure is taken as an indication of the value added by carving ivory within Hong Kong. It must be noted that these calculations do not take into account any costs of worked ivory production within Hong Kong, such as labour costs. Nor do the estimates account for the value of the ivory indirectly exported through tourist sales and worked ivory consumed domestically. In the early 1980s this estimated added value amounted to approximately $15–19 million annually. Since then it has increased to well over $20 million each year, reaching a peak of $28 million in 1985. Between 1979 and 1988 the estimated value added by carving ivory in Hong

Table 3.2: The value of the worked ivory trade: Hong Kong, 1978–87 (in thousand US$)

Year	Worked ivory imports	Worked ivory exports	Worked ivory re-exports	Net raw ivory imports	Total exports less total imports
1978	4,310.3	29,568.6	NA	19,373.2	5,885.1
1979	4,712.0	29,806.5	2,499.5	17,706.5	9,887.6
1980	5,219.5	39,288.6	2,119.0	18,347.1	17,841.0
1981	3,929.6	34,075.1	1,443.3	12,886.3	18,702.6
1982	2,886.6	26,092.2	1,603.5	8,571.1	16,238.1
1983	3,000.9	29,588.0	1,198.7	12,356.8	15,429.0
1984	3,377.6	38,719.0	1,127.7	12,025.5	24,443.0
1985	5,018.5	35,077.1	1,436.3	3,534.9	27,960.0
1986	6,994.4	34,359.2	1,782.7	6,652.0	22,495.5
1987	7,900.4	36,246.0	1,783.2	7,906.9	22,221.9

Source: Based on customs import and export data for Hong Kong.

Kong is well over $180 million.

In recent years, the carving industry in Hong Kong appears to be in a state of decline: both imports of raw ivory and exports of worked ivory have declined since 1985. This can be attributed to two key factors: first, Hong Kong's dependance upon Africa as its ultimate source of raw ivory supplies; and, second, Hong Kong's dependance upon international demand for worked ivory, and especially upon a few principal consuming countries. This second factor means that Hong Kong is very vulnerable to changes in importing countries' regulations and also to changing consumer tastes – over which Hong Kong is unable to have any real influence. The key factors in the international supply and demand that influence Hong Kong's role in the ivory trade can be summarized as:

i)   the downward trend in the supply of ivory from Africa;
ii)   strict trade regulations imposed on export markets;
iii) changing consumer tastes towards purchasing ivory; and
iv)   the impending reversion of Hong Kong to China in 1997.[4]

One of the outcomes of these factors has been an inability to recruit new carvers into the industry in Hong Kong.

Hong Kong's role as re-exporter of raw ivory is facing a similar decline. As noted above, this re-exporting role is based upon Hong

Kong's ablility to sort ivory shipments and re-export the large tusks. However, it is increasingly difficult to get hold of shipments containing large tusks because older male elephants are now very rare. As a result, shipments in recent years have contained a much reduced assortment of tusk size and quality. Instead, they have been made up of mainly small tusks from female and young elephants. Consequently, Hong Kong is no longer able to sort the tusks and to re-export ivory according to the specific requirements of the importing country, Thus, its previous advantage in supplying ivory has diminished. Hong Kong is increasingly likely to retain all the ivory it can obtain for its own carving industries, and Japan and China are likely to try to establish direct trading links with the African ivory-producing countries.

Japan

Japan is the second largest importer of raw ivory after Hong Kong. Japan, in contrast to Hong Kong, relies upon intermediary ivory traders, especially Hong Kong and Belgium, for the majority of its raw ivory imports. Japan consumes most of this raw ivory in its ivory-carving industry, producing goods mainly to satisfy its domestic demand. Between 1979 and 1987 gross and net imports of raw ivory into Japan accounted for 38 per cent and 32 per cent respectively of the total world trade in raw ivory. Japan's gross imports of raw ivory increased from around 300–400 tonnes in the 1970s to as much as 465 tonnes in 1983 and 1984. However, for a number of reasons, including compliance with CITES regulations from 1985–6, raw ivory imports declined to under 300 tonnes in 1985, and from 1986 onwards gross raw ivory imports have levelled at around 110 tonnes annually, according to Japanese customs statistics. Again, Chapter 4 will analyse in more detail the Japanese raw ivory trade.

Prior to the 1970s, imports into Japan mainly came directly from the African producing states.[5] However, in the 1970s, some of the trading routes of raw ivory into Japan were diverted through intermediary countries, including Hong Kong and European nations. As mentioned previously, this was due partly to the special relationship that Japan and Hong Kong developed over raw ivory transactions, and also to the connections established between African and European traders.[6]

Throughout the 1980s Japan increasingly relied upon these intermediary countries for its raw ivory imports. The share of the individual countries supplying these imports has been fluctuating for three years from 1986–8, as shown in Table 3.3.

Hong Kong's share of total imports into Japan averaged 40 per

Table 3.3: Percentage of Japanese raw ivory imports from major traders, 1986–88

Year	Hong Kong	Belgium	Singapore	African Producers	Others
1986	40.7	36.6	–	13.8	8.9
1987	24.2	20.6	29.8	22.0	3.4
1988	62.2	9.7	22.3	1.8	3.4
1986–88	40.5	20.9	20.3	13.6	4.7

Source: T. Milliken, "The Japanese Ivory Trade: Tradition, CITES, and the Elusive Search for Sustainable Utilisation" from the ITRG Report, *The Ivory Trade and the Future of the African Elephant* (1989)

cent between 1986–8, although in 1988 Hong Kong monopolized over 60 per cent of the raw import trade into Japan.[7] European nations played a dominant role, Belgium in particular, with an average import share of around 20.5 per cent between 1986–8, although declining to 10 per cent in 1988. Singapore recently developed its role as an ivory entrepôt, and established a high profile by accounting for 20–30 per cent of raw ivory imports into Japan in 1987–8. Between 1986 and 1988, only 13.6 per cent of the raw ivory imports into Japan were imported directly from African producing countries.

The origin of these tusks has been predominantly from Congo, Central African Republic, Zaire and Sudan. Since 1971 these four countries have been the source of around 70 per cent of the total imports of the raw ivory entering Japan – the remainder has come mainly from Uganda, South Africa and Tanzania.[8]

Japan is the major worked ivory-consuming country. It consumes approximately 38 per cent of all worked ivory produced throughout the world with the remainder split between the EEC (18 per cent), the USA (16 per cent) and other Asian countries.[9] Imports of raw ivory into Japan have been used mainly for domestic consumption in the ivory-carving industry, with little entrepôt trade of any significance. Japan does export to Hong Kong some scraps of raw ivory that are left over from its ivory-carving industry and are considered of little use within Japan.

Japan's ivory-carving industry can be divided into five categories according to the goods produced:

i)   seals;
ii) parts of musical instruments;

   iii) sculptures;
   iv) jewellery; and,
   v)   other accessories, e.g. chopsticks, cigarette holders, etc.

The production of name seals (which are used instead of signatures in Japan) is the major use of ivory in Japan. Approximately 64 per cent of total net imports of raw ivory into Japan is consumed in this industry.[10] Therefore, approximately 25 per cent of the world consumption of raw ivory is used in the production of seals in Japan. To give some idea of the magnitude of this use, between 1977–87, 1,841 tonnes of the total net imports of raw ivory of 2,832 tonnes were used in seal production. Of the rest, approximately 12 per cent is consumed in the production of parts of musical instruments, such as piano keys and guitar parts, 6 per cent in sculpture and netsukes. What remains, plus any scraps that are left over from the other industries, is either consumed in the jewellery and accessories industries or exported to Hong Kong.

    The vast majority of worked ivory produced by Japanese carvers remains within Japan to serve domestic demand. There are also some imports of worked ivory entering into Japan (see Table 3.4). Hong Kong is the principal source of worked ivory imports entering Japan, and accounts for approximately 80 per cent of total worked ivory imports. Other countries from which Japan receives worked ivory include China, India, Thailand, Taiwan and occasionally the USA and the EEC. In 1988 Japan received a large shipment of worked ivory from Singapore. During the period 1979–87 the value of imports of worked ivory into Japan each year was approximately $200,000. There has been a steady increase in the value of worked ivory imports from $100,000 in 1979 to a peak of $360,000 in 1983. After 1983 there was a brief decline in imports, but by 1987 the value of imports of worked ivory into Japan again reached $200,000.

    Individuals working within the ivory industry in Japan – including manufacturers, carvers and retailers – have traditionally belonged to organizations specifically established for ivory-linked occupations.[11] In December 1984 a new organization was established by Japan ivory importers – the Japan Ivory Importers Association (JIIA). This was set up because a number of critical challenges facing ivory importers came to the fore. First, there was severe domestic and international criticism of Japan's import policies, second, the advent of CITES, and third, a growing awareness that illegal trade practices would undermine the long-term survival of the industry. The majority of Japanese importers are members of JIIA, and since 1986 about 90 per cent of all ivory trade has passed through the Association. JIIA

Table 3.4: The value of the worked ivory trade: Japan, 1978–87 (in thousand US$)

Year	Worked ivory imports	Worked ivory exports
1978	94.1	1,600.9
1979	111.8	1,072.3
1980	151.8	1,088.5
1981	176.0	1,194.8
1982	172.7	826.4
1983	359.9	652.0
1984	237.8	531.6
1985	167.4	529.7
1986	184.7	956.1
1987	223.3	623.1

Source: Based on customs import and export data for Japan.

members have agreed to allocate 1.2 per cent of the value of each ivory transaction to a central fund which is to be used at their discretion. So far, money generated in this way has been donated to the CITES Secretariat's Ivory Fund and other conservation activities, and has provided financial support for attendance at CITES conferences.

Japan exports little worked ivory and these exports have been declining in recent years. Table 3.4 shows the value of worked ivory exports from Japan between 1978–87 to the rest of the world, but especially to the USA and Europe. Total exports of worked ivory have fluctuated from a peak of $1,330,000 in 1981 to a low of $500,000 in 1984–5. In 1987 they rested at $600,000.

In 1981 Martin estimated the annual retail value of finished ivory products in Japan to be worth between $200 million and $250 million.[12] In particular, the two million business seals carved annually (averaging $90 each) account for as much as $180 million. Martin noted that this total retail value of finished ivory products in Japan is worth more than the entire gross national product of some African countries.

Trade Flows and Final Demand: Europe

Europe has played an important role in the international trade of elephant ivory, with some countries in particular acting as staging posts for raw ivory from Africa on its way to Hong Kong and Asia. Europe has also consumed significant quantities of worked ivory and, although some ivory carving is undertaken, ivory-carving industries comparable to those of Japan and Hong Kong have not been established.

Belgium

Belgium has traditionally been a major ivory-trading country. Although Belgium dealt with significant quantities of raw ivory, it never developed a substantial ivory-processing industry – it was principally a staging post between Africa and Asia. In recent years, as noted in Appendix 2.1, customs statistics have not reflected the true volume of ivory passing through Belgium, as much of this was held in bonded warehouses and never entered customs statistics. Belgium trade statistics suggest that it imported 369 tonnes of ivory between 1979–84. Transit statistics suggest that 840 tonnes may have come through Belgium during this period. However, importing countries record at least 1,500 tons of ivory as re-exported from Belgium during 1979–84.[13]

Belgium's dominant role as a staging post for raw ivory en route to Asia until the mid 1980s was based upon expertise that was established in handling the ivory cargo, an ability to communicate with both the African producers and the Asian consumers, and, of major importance, the virtual absence of trade controls on shipments in and out of Belgium. During the 1970s traders from the ivory-producing countries established Belgium as a base from which to sell their ivory. Later, in the early 1980s, two major Asian ivory entrepreneurs based themselves in Belgium to establish direct links to the major African exporters. These entrepreneurs were able to deal directly with the producing countries, effectively bypassing Belgian middlemen.

In 1984 strict measures to regulate the trade in elephant ivory were imposed in Belgium. All ivory passing through the country requires valid CITES documentation and strict enforcement is carried out. Faced with these severe trade regulations, the Asian entrepreneurs pulled out of Belgium. Having already established direct links with the African producers they were able to continue trading with them from Asia without the staging point of Belgium. Belgium and its domestic ivory traders suffered a significant decline. Little, if any, illegal and a much reduced legal ivory trade continues through Belgium.

The United Kingdom and West Germany

The United Kingdom and West Germany have traditionally traded in raw ivory mainly as a commodity for re-export, and have been a significant stepping stone in the international ivory-trading route between Africa and Asia. They did not develop substantial processing industries, and although they consumed some worked ivory this was not highly significant. In recent years, their role in the ivory trade has declined. Presently, the UK deals with around 20 tonnes of raw ivory per annum, consuming 3–4 tonnes of this domestically for piano keys, mounts for bagpipes and so on.[14] The rest is re-exported, mainly to Hong Kong, Japan and India.

Worked ivory imports into the UK are given in Table 3.5.[15] From 1978 it is apparent that the imports have been steadily declining, from 23 tonnes worth £382,000 in 1979, and 17 tonnes worth £487,000 in 1980, to under 1 tonne worth £241,000 in 1987. The majority of these imports have come from Hong Kong. Between 1978 and 1987 inclusive, the quantity of worked ivory imports into the UK has been less than 65 tonnes.

West Germany regularly imported around 20–30 tonnes of raw ivory per annum in the early 1980s. This declined to below 10 tonnes each year in the latter half of the 1980s, and less than 4 tonnes in 1987. Exports of raw ivory have also declined, from less than 4 tonnes in the early 1980s, to less than 1 tonne in recent years. Worked-ivory trade has declined dramatically, with imports over 20 tonnes in 1979–81

Table 3.5: Worked ivory imports into the UK, 1978–87

Year	kg	£
1978	5,603	267,062
1979	22,760	381,931
1980	17,217	487,052
1981	2,984	237,566
1982	4,576	262,854
1983	4,743	310,918
1984	2,856	454,779
1985	1,065	266,665
1986	1,797	251,567
1987	842	240,934

Source: Based on customs import and export data for the UK.

falling to just over 2 tonnes in 1987, and exports falling from around 3 tonnes to 0.3 tonnes during the same period.

France

Although France owned the African ivory lands of the Central African Republic, Cameroon, Senegal, Ivory Coast and others, it never really developed an entrepôt trade comparable to that of Belgium, the UK or West Germany.[16] In recent years, France has been receiving raw ivory, principally from Congo, Tanzania, Gabon and Chad, in total quantities of around 5–15 tonnes per annum. France did develop ivory-processing industries, although in recent years these too have declined. Imports of worked ivory are mainly from Hong Kong, China and India. In recent years, France has also received worked ivory imports directly from African producing nations, in particular Kenya, but also from the countries noted above with whom France established traditional raw ivory trading links. Exports of worked ivory from France are mainly transported to the USA and other European countries.

Trade Flows and Final Demand: USA

The USA is not a major consumer of raw ivory, but is a major consumer of worked ivory. United States customs statistics categorize raw elephant ivory imports under "raw ivory". This category includes a range of ivories – including whale, hippopotamus, walrus and mammoth "ivory" along with elephant ivory. The categorization does not specify what sort of ivory is being imported. In the 1950s and 1960s, imports of raw ivory into the USA comprised mainly a mixture of raw elephant ivory and sperm whale teeth. Although African elephant ivory originally accounted for a dominant share of total raw ivory imports in the 1950s – just under 90 per cent – this position was gradually undermined by an increasing percentage of sperm whale ivory during the 1960s and early 1970s.[17] African elephant ivory declined to less than 20 per cent of the total imports of raw ivory by the early 1970s.

In 1973 the USA banned imports of sperm whale ivory as this species became classified as endangered under the US Endangered Species Act. However, the total level of all raw ivory imports remained constant at around 16 tonnes. This suggested that other ivories were used as substitutes for whale ivory, in particular African elephant ivory. In the late 1970s raw ivory imports fluctuated dramatically, peaking at 35 tonnes in 1976, whilst throughout the 1980s raw ivory imports remained more consistent at around 4–8 tonnes a year. In the late 1980s imports declined, especially after 1986 with the introduction of the CITES African Elephant Ivory Quota Control System.

The USA is probably the world's largest importer of elephant skins. The majority of skins are used for boot manufacture in Texas. Although the trade in skins has not been analysed, the USA's total consumption is likely to be approximately equal to that of Europe. Together these countries account for the vast majority of the market for elephant skins.[18] The trade in elephant skins appears to be significantly different from the trade in elephant ivory. In the case of skins, the supply comes mainly from southern African nations including Zimbabwe, South Africa and Botswana. These skins are obtained from culling operations that are carried out within these countries to manage their elephant populations. There is little, if any, illegal poaching of elephant skins.

Thomsen records that, according to industry representatives, the average annual quantity of skins imported into the USA is approximately $500,000 \text{ ft}^2$ from over 11,000 elephants. However, this figure is likely to be too high, and estimates from the culling operations of Zimbabwe, South Africa and Botswana suggest that the total number of elephants involved in supplying skins for all the international trade was around 7,000. The declared import value of the trade in 1986 was over $1 million. These exports may be of great significance to the producer countries – the total annual export revenue generated from exports of elephant skins from Zimbabwe amounts to $2 million.

Like most of Europe, the USA has not developed an ivory-processing industry and has relied upon those of Hong Kong, Japan, China and India for worked ivory products. However, some ivory processing does exist – for example, carving of pistol handles in New Mexico and Texas, and traditional American scrimshaw manufacturing in Alaska, Hawaii and New England. The demand for worked ivory in the USA has declined since 1986 as substitutes, such as plastic, are increasingly being used in place of ivory. For example, plastics are used for producing billiard balls, piano keys, pistol grips and knife handles rather than the traditional raw material of elephant ivory.[19] Also, other substitute ivories are also being used, such as walrus, hippopotamus or whale ivory, and also mammoth ivory. However, the texture and size of elephant ivory still makes it the preferable choice of raw material for carving and producing scrimshaw scenes.

The small quantities of raw ivory that are required for the USA domestic carving industry have been increasingly difficult to obtain in recent years. High ivory prices and the time-consuming paperwork associated with importing ivory has deterred imports of raw ivory into the USA. Since late 1988 the USA prohibited re-exports of raw ivory, compounding disincentives to trade in African elephant ivory. One result is that the ivory-processing industry has recently been purchasing raw ivory from domestic stocks held in the USA. These are made up of both trophy collections and ivory held for investment purposes. These stocks may be at least 80 tonnes and could sustain the present level of raw ivory consumption for at least ten years.

The USA has traditionally been a major consumer of worked ivory.[20] Thomsen estimated that during the mid-1980s, consumption of ivory there amounted to approximately 10-12 per cent of all ivory traded throughout the world.[21] The USA imports the majority of its worked ivory from Hong Kong. This source accounts for over 90 per cent of the total value of worked ivory imports into the USA. Up until 1987 it was the largest export market for ivory manufactured in Hong Kong, and in 1985 and 1986 consumed around 45 per cent of Hong Kong's total worked ivory exports. However, in 1987 imports of worked ivory into Japan surpassed those into USA, although the USA still continued to import over 30 per cent of Hong Kong's exports.

The structure of the ivory-importing industry within the USA is concentrated between a few major traders. The five largest ivory importers are Chinese families who have been in the business for over twenty years. Between them they account for between 40-80 per cent of all sales of worked ivory in the USA.[22] Some of these entrepreneurs also have connections in the ivory retail industry within the USA. The majority of imports are made up of jewellery and sculptures, although a diverse range of other goods includes plates in the handles of carving knives, other utensils and belt buckles.

During the period 1984-8 the average annual import value of worked ivory into the USA was over $26 million and this corresponds to an average retail value of $100 million. However, there are indications that the ivory trade there is declining. Up until 1986 imports of worked ivory were increasing, peaking at 8,500,000 pieces and 4.4 tonnes in 1986. After 1986, the quantity of carved ivory pieces imported has decreased to 1,450,000 pieces and 22.2 tonnes. Although there has been a decrease in the volume of imports, the value appears to have increased – the average price per piece of worked ivory has risen from $6.3 in 1984 to $14.9 in 1988.

The major causes of depressed demand are:

i)   rising ivory prices;
ii)   cheaper substitutes;

iii) public opinion;
iv) changing jewellery fashions; and,
v) alternative investments to ivory are expected to produce higher returns.

As mentioned previously, alternative materials are available to replace most of the uses of raw elephant ivory in the manufacturing industry in the USA. The rising price of ivory and the relative difficulty of importing has discouraged transactions to import raw elephant ivory. There is great uncertainty and risk involved in holding ivory as an investment and the financial incentives are unlikely to be sufficient to offset this. Thus, ivory stocks held for investment purposes are currently being released to the domestic market and used in the ivory-processing industry.

Public opinion is becoming a dominant factor in the declining USA demand for ivory products. Throughout 1988 and 1989 there were intensive campaigns to alert the public to the threat of extinction of the African elephant.[23] As in the case of the fur trade, the approach was essentially very emotive and based upon moral arguments. The campaigns took a variety of forms, including public appeals, newspaper articles, books, television coverage and direct-mail fund-raising letters. These campaigns have had a significant impact upon attitudes towards buying ivory, which is strongly undermining the demand.

Trade Flows and Final Demand: China

China is a major importer of raw ivory that is used to supply the raw material input to its large domestic carving industry. The majority of China's raw ivory imports have, in the past, come through the intermediary staging points of Hong Kong and Belgium. Data from Hong Kong's customs statistics indicate that around 25 tonnes of raw ivory were re-exported annually to China in the early 1980s.[24] The Chinese have established trading links with Hong Kong because, like Japan, they prefer the larger, better quality tusks and, rather than having to purchase a mixture of ivory sold in lots, they have been able to select individual pieces of ivory from the Hong Kong traders.

Chinese customs statistics, for the period from 1981 to 1987 inclusive, indicate that the total quantity of ivory imports during this time amounted to just over 185 tonnes at a value of approximately $16 million (see Table 3.6). This gives an estimated level of imports of 31 tonnes at a value of $2.6 million each year. However, estimates of imports of raw ivory from all sources (including illegal) suggest that at

Table 3.6: The ivory trade in China, 1981-87

Year	Imports: raw ivory Quantity (kg)	Value (US$)	Exports: worked ivory Value (US$)
1981	14,698	1,069,389	6,354,099
1982	53,798	4,280,808	5,278,240
1983	20,497	1,457,675	6,049,377
1984	13,528	784,869	5,629,797
1985	9,888	596,991	5,347,214
1986	23,604	1,670,140	4,172,171
1987	50,160	6,231,603	446,914
Total	186,173	16,091,475	33,277,812

Source: Based on Chinese customs statistics. Dollar calculations made courtesy of Wildlife Trade Monitoring Unit.

least 30 tonnes of raw ivory is annually imported into China.[25] Exports of raw ivory during the 1980s, according to Chinese customs data, were nominal. China also imports some worked ivory, mainly from Hong Kong. The average annual importation of worked ivory between 1983-6 was valued at $275 thousand.

The Chinese ivory-carving industry is the third largest in the world behind those of Japan and Hong Kong, in terms of both the quantity of raw ivory consumed and number of craftsmen. In 1985, China was estimated to have between 1,200 and 1,600 ivory craftsmen, carving or manufacturing ivory jewellery, statues and other artefacts. In comparison, in 1985 Hong Kong had 1,200 employees directly engaged in ivory processing, whilst in 1979 India had an estimated 7,200[26] and Japan 2,800.[27]

Over 98 per cent of all ivory manufactured in China is exported, mainly to Hong Kong and some to Japan, the USA and Europe.[28] Table 3.6 gives the value of worked ivory exports from China, based on Chinese customs statistics from 1981 up until 1987. The total value of worked ivory exports during this time amounted to $33 million, giving average annual export earnings of nearly $5.5 million. Of this, 62 per cent of total exports went to Hong Kong, and 10 per cent went to the USA. Hong Kong's customs data show that the total value of all worked ivory imports from China into Hong Kong amounted to $32 million between 1979 to 1988. The value of imports has increased from $3.5 million in 1979 to $5 million in 1988. The value of the worked ivory is often at least twice the value of the raw ivory imports, although it can be up to five times the value for intricate carvings.[29]

Domestic consumption of worked ivory is low in China, mainly because of the high price of the finished products. Seals (used in place of signatures) made of ivory are four times as much as those made of stone in China, and just less than double those made of jade. The majority of the remaining ivory carvings are sold in tourist hotel shops, especially to Japanese visitors. Although there has been an increase in the number of foreign tourists - especially Japanese, Western Europeans and North Americans who are the major buyers of worked ivory - sales, particularly of large items, have been decreasing recently. This is partly due to the reduced availability of good quality raw ivory at a reasonable price that has translated into fewer, more expensive carvings of worked ivory, but also due to the strict regulations of customs controls and CITES and the change in Western tourists' attitudes towards buying ivory.

Trade Flows and Final Demand: India

Indian elephant ivory was traditionally used for carving in India. It was not until the nineteenth century that significant quantities of African ivory was imported.[30] The Indian ivory is much harder than the African and because of this characteristic, Indian elephant ivory is preferred by Japanese carvers. However, Indian carvers tended to prefer the softer African ivory as the tusks were often larger, less brittle and easier for carving. Thus, India exported ivory to Japan in the early 1900s, whilst at the same time importing ivory from Africa for domestic processing.

In 1976 India became a party to CITES, and from then onwards exports of Indian ivory and products containing this ivory were technically illegal as the Indian elephant was classified as an endangered species. Enforcement of such regulations was extremely difficult as the authorities had severe problems in distinguishing between African and Indian ivory. This confusion led to much bureaucracy and paperwork.

In India the maximum number of elephants remaining in the wild is estimated to be approximately 22,000, and the minimum 16,500, with around 3,000 elephants held for domestic use.[31] Although there is concern about the poaching of elephant ivory in India, especially in the south, elephant numbers in India are on the increase.

India's importance in the international African elephant ivory market fluctuated during the twentieth century. India was the largest ivory market prior to World War I and for a brief period after World War II. However, this dominant position in the ivory trade was gradually undermined by Hong Kong and Japan – a situation that remains unchanged today. A much reduced availability of ivory from Africa led to India importing ivory from Hong Kong at a much inflated price in the late 1970s.

Between 1980 and 1987 inclusive, annual imports of African elephant ivory were only 13.24 tonnes according to customs data, and 9.46 tonnes according to CITES statistics.[32] However, India imposed severe trade duties on ivory imports of 120 per cent in 1978 which later rose to 140 per cent. Although this added to the supply constraints and the costs of importing ivory into India, these policies also created a significant incentive for illegal importation of raw ivory, and incorrect customs and CITES documentation. Illegal imports may have been transported from Dubai, UAE, Tanzania and Singapore. It is likely that total imports, made up of both legal and illegal transactions, are substantially greater than those that are recorded by CITES and customs import statistics.

India's strict domestic policy towards African elephant ivory has further hampered the trade. The Indian CITES Management Authority surpassed the requirements of the CITES Secretariat when Singapore joined CITES in 1987 – and refused to allow the legalized imports of Singapore's ivory into India. This decision was taken on the basis that this ivory had no valid country-of-origin documentation and was highly likely to have come from illegal sources. These Singapore stocks were later bought up by Hong Kong, China and Japan. A further policy of the Indian CITES Authority is that, for political reasons, ivory from South Africa is not allowed to be imported into India. These policies have effectively denied Indian traders access to substantial supplies of ivory.

In 1986 in response to the pressures on the Indian elephant from poaching, the Indian government banned all trade in Indian ivory within the country. Later, in 1988, they abolished all import duties on African ivory imports into India. This was to prevent further decline in the Indian elephant population that might arise due to a trade-off between the African and Indian elephant ivory. Implementation of the 1986 ban requires detailed documentation to ensure that the ivory dealings within the country are of African origin only. Tourists are required to obtain export permits for carvings that they purchase whilst in India. This procedure is extremely complicated and time consuming and a significant deterrent for any tourist wishing to purchase ivory. The issuing of annual licenses for all ivory factories, dealers, exporters and carvers, is combined with periodic inspections.

All these factors have severely constrained the ivory industry in India, which is now experiencing a serious decline.

What little ivory-carving industry remains in India has shifted away from the traditional, elaborate and time-consuming carving to the production of relatively less expensive and less detailed tourist trinkets. The majority of worked ivory is destined for the export markets of the USA and the rest for Europe. Recently, links have been established with Japanese traders by changes being made in the style of carving to suit Asian demand. The major purchases of the more expensive items of carved ivory tend to be by Gulf Arabs. A rough estimate of the wholesale value of India's ivory exports amounts to $15 million, although this is a minimum estimate and does not account for all illegal imports/exports.[33]

Trade Flows and Final Demand: Other Countries

This section outlines the flow of trade and the final demand in any of the ivory-trading countries not discussed previously. In doing so it reflects the remarkable fluid nature of the ivory trade. As various regulations have been imposed to contain illicit ivory transactions, different diversion tactics have arisen – from shifting imports from raw to worked ivory to shifting the country staging points to accommodate the varying country regulations. Underlying these movements there is a complicated interlinkage between key traders from Hong Kong and newly established carving centres. The constancy of the connections between the major participants contrasts with the fluidity of the transactions.

Macau

Macau's role in the ivory trade dramatically emerged in the early 1980s.[34] Macau began exporting relatively insignificant volumes of worked ivory to Hong Kong from 1981 (see Table 3.7). Thereafter, the industry grew rapidly with imports of raw ivory increasing from around 5 tonnes in 1982 to over 80 tonnes in 1985 and just under 60 tonnes in 1986 (see Table 1.3). In 1985–6 Macau accounted for 10–15 per cent of world consumption of raw ivory. The majority of this ivory is believed to have come from illicit sources.

This dramatic increase in raw ivory imports was induced by the activities of certain Hong Kong traders, who were attempting to avoid the CITES trade restrictions that were constraining their domestic activities. In order to avoid the strict restrictions on trade in ivory in Hong Kong, the traders looked for other countries to act as staging points. Although Macau was considered a party to CITES by

Table 3.7: Value of Hong Kong's worked ivory imports from Macau, Singapore, Taiwan and United Arab Emirates, 1979–88 (US$)

Year	Macau	Singapore	Taiwan	United Arab Emirates
1979	0	9,757	33,041	4,081
1980	0	4,444	6.097	4,148
1981	95,455	2,201	2,963	0
1982	190,154	8,023	6,582	0
1983	135,888	12,277	540	0
1984	126,433	9,133	5,447	1,549
1985	664,486	125,071	848	0
1986	1,830,813	916,536	0	0
1987	1,379,903	2,070,372	221,105	461,613
1988	827,979	0	77,451	1,168,235

Source: Derived from Hong Kong customs statistics. See T. Milliken and D. Melvin, Appendix to "The Hong Kong Ivory Trade", June 1989, Draft Report to the Second Meeting of the CITES African Elephant Working Group, Gabarone, Botswana, (July 1989).

virtue of Portugal's accession to the Convention in 1981, it engaged in illegal ivory trading in the early 1980s. Hong Kong traders were quick to take up this opportunity and shift some of their illicit dealings to this country. By mid-1984, at least ten factories had been established by Hong Kong dealers in Macau. Imports of worked ivory into Hong Kong from Macau increased to a peak value of $1.8 million in 1986.

International pressure on Macau to stop dealing in illicit ivory eventually emerged in January 1986. The CITES Secretariat called for a total ban on Macau's wildlife trade, and in February 1986 this finally came into force. However, rather than quell the activities of the traders, it merely induced them to shift their operations to another country that was not overtly responsive to their illicit activities. As a result, many of the Macau carvers, including those that were employed by the Hong Kong dealers, moved to factories in Singapore to continue production.

Singapore
After the ivory route through Macau was effectively closed off, Singapore emerged as the new staging point for illicit ivory from Africa on its way to Hong Kong. Singapore was relatively unimpor-

tant in the ivory trade until 1984 when net consumption of raw ivory suddenly rose dramatically. Net raw ivory imports reached 120 tonnes in 1984, then fell to 60 tonnes in 1985 and rose again to as much as 324 tonnes in 1986 (see Table 1.3).[35] As in the case of Macau, certain Hong Kong dealers apparently either colluded with local manufacturers to increase production or established their own carving factories within Singapore.

Since 1984 the CITES Secretariat has attempted to discourage trade with Singapore, and, although this may have been effective in the following year, in 1986 Singapore accounted for almost 55 per cent of total world consumption of raw ivory (see Table 1.4). Although between 1982 and 1986, Hong Kong customs statistics indicate no imports of raw ivory from Singapore in compliance with CITES guidelines, there were no restrictions on trade in manufactured products. The value of worked-ivory imports into Hong Kong from Singapore rose dramatically after 1984, from less than $10 thousand in 1984 to $125 thousand in 1985, $917 thousand in 1986 and a substantial $2.1 million in 1987 (see Table 3.7). In 1988, after strict regulations were finally imposed in Hong Kong on illicit imports of worked ivory, there were no further imports of worked ivory from Singapore into Hong Kong.

Although the ivory-processing industry increased dramatically throughout the mid-1980s in Singapore, the level of raw ivory imports surpassed the capacity of the industry to consume it. Large stockpiles built up. In November 1986, Singapore joined CITES and thus dealings in ivory not sanctioned by CITES were supposedly halted. At the time of joining CITES, stockpiles of ivory from mostly illicit sources that had been amassed within Singapore amounted to some 300 tonnes. Upon joining CITES, these stocks of ivory were given legitimate registration by CITES and were later exported legally. The price of this previously illicit ivory was originally around $50/kg. However, once the ivory had been declared legitimate the price doubled. Quick profits of as much as $77.5 million are likely to have been made on these stocks.[36] The majority of these raw ivory stocks were owned by Hong Kong traders and were later shipped to Hong Kong.

Taiwan

Restricting the ivory trade through Singapore did not deter the traders: it simply deflected their base from Singapore, and before that Macau, to Taiwan. Historically, Taiwan has had a small ivory-carving industry importing around 15 tonnes of raw ivory annually, mainly for domestic processing for internal consumption and some exports.[37] Taiwan also imported small quantities of worked ivory, mainly from Hong Kong and China (via Hong Kong). During the period 1981–7, imports of worked ivory from Hong Kong and China (via Hong Kong) remained consistently low, valued around $1,000 per annum. Worked ivory exports in the early 1980s averaged around $10–12,000 for 10–15 tonnes.

Worked ivory exports dramatically increased in 1987 to $894,754 at a total weight of 38 tonnes. To sustain this new level of trade, imports of raw ivory increased over five times their usual level, exceeding 80 tonnes at a cost of $2,378. This dramatic increase appears to have been induced by an equally rapid expansion of the domestic carving industry. Once again, entrepreneurs from Hong Kong established new factories and brought in carvers from Hong Kong to undertake the extra work. Prior to 1986 little or no trade in worked ivory had been recorded between Hong Kong and Taiwan. However, in 1987, worked ivory imports jumped to $221,000 (see Table 3.7).

This activity caused considerable alarm that Taiwan (a non-Party to CITES) was rapidly emerging as ''the new hub for illegal trade and ivory processing in Asia''.[38] In response to this a series of strict measures was rapidly undertaken to restrict the trade. China instigated comprehensive controls on ivory trading in Taiwan, including licenses for all imports of raw and worked ivory which require valid CITES export permits before the submission of the import documentation. Re-exports of raw and worked ivory also require a valid license. As a further measure to discourage trade, tariffs were levied, ranging from 5–20 per cent on the declared value of raw ivory imports.

These drastic measures appear to have been effective, at least for trade through Taiwan, as raw ivory imports into Taiwan dropped below 6 tonnes in 1988, and worked ivory exports to Hong Kong from Taiwan declined to $77,000 in 1988, according to customs data. The individuals who were temporarily assigned to Taiwan as ivory carvers have since left, and the domestic ivory-carving industry is experiencing a serious decline. However, although there is an inauspicious future for Taiwan's domestic ivory carving and ivory trade, demand for worked ivory in Taiwan has not been eradicated. Imports of worked ivory have been steadily increasing in recent years and by 1988 they were worth some $300,000.

Dubai and the United Arab Emirates

The role of the United Arab Emirates (UAE) as an illicit ivory staging point came to the fore as those of Macau, Singapore and Taiwan were gradually closed off. The UAE repudiated the Convention on International Trade in Endangered Species in January 1988. They are the only members of CITES to have withdrawn from it altogether. As in the previous examples, ivory manufacturing factories were set up in Dubai. These were established in collaboration with the complex, transient network of traders from Hong Kong and carvers that had shifted from country to country to evade the trade restrictions on illicit ivory.

Again, as is typical in the previously mentioned countries, Dubai had no significant history in ivory carving and trading. Up until 1986 there were few, if any, recorded tradings between the UAE and Hong Kong. Then, suddenly, in 1987 worked ivory imports into Hong Kong rose to $462,000 from UAE and then increased further to $1,168,000 in 1988 (Table 3.7). In late 1988, following China's lead, legislation in Hong Kong was finally passed which banned all ivory transactions with the UAE.

Conclusion

The traditional ivory trading and carving centres have, in most cases, been declining in recent years due to the low availability of African elephant ivory coupled with a high price and compounded by changing Western consumer tastes away from ivory products, and increasing restrictions on imports/exports of ivory. However, it is not clear that the international trade in elephant ivory is declining at the rate that the decline in the traditional major consuming nations would suggest. There have been some very determined attempts to maintain trade in elephant ivory that have resulted in rapid shifts of trade and carving centres between countries in attempts to avoid increasingly strict ivory trade controls.

The determination and ability of a few major ivory traders to continue trading, given the increasingly strict trade restrictions, suggests that the demand for ivory is creating sufficient financial incentives to continue the trade. However, the demand for elephant ivory may have shifted away from the more traditional ivory-consuming centres of the West to a more diversified range of developing economies, for example, South Korea, China and Taiwan. The link between demand for ivory and increasing real income levels is discussed in the following chapter, where the demand for ivory in Hong Kong and Japan is analysed in greater detail.

Appendix 3.1: Worked Ivory Database

Collecting and compiling statistics of worked ivory imports and exports of countries engaged in trade is fraught with difficulties. First of all, there is a problem of lack of available data. Often the data are incomplete, if they are available at all, especially for some of the less developed countries. In particular, current statistics are rarely available. The majority of worked ivory data was obtained from the library at the UK Department of Trade and Industry. However, when the required customs statistics were not available from this source, direct requests in writing were made to the Customs Office of the country in question. The data collected were compiled onto a database, listing the country of import, the country of export, the year, the quantity of ivory traded in kg, and the value of the worked ivory transaction in the original currency and also converted to US dollars.

To illustrate the complexities of undertaking this database to determine the trade in worked ivory, a brief overview of India's customs trade statistics of worked ivory in 1986 are examined in Table 3.8.

The most obvious difficulty is that there are many gaps in the India data. Values are generally given, but volumes are not always available. A second problem is that Indian customs statistics are given in years running from April to March, whereas the majority of other countries use the calendar year, running from January to December. This causes problems for cross-country comparisons. To bring Indian's statistical year in line with the majority it may be possible to obtain data for January to March and data for April to December and then recalculate a January to December year for India. However, India's data is notoriously difficult to get hold of, especially for individual months as well as March year-ends, and in practice this method is unrealistic.

A further major problem is the classification of ivory. There is no one consistent category for worked ivory – India classes ivory under a number of headings: "worked ivory and articles thereof", "ivory manufactured as artware", and a further category not listed above, "wood inlaid with ivory, metal, etc". The volume and value of ivory varies between the individual ivory articles, both across the classes and within the classes. For example, "worked ivory and articles thereof" may contain ivory carvings made of ivory only; these may be small or large pieces and be relatively cheap or very expensive. "Ivory manufactured as artware" is likely to include jewellery that contains a mixture of ivory and other precious materials, such as gold and silver, again with a variety of percentages of volume and a range of values. "Wood inlaid with ivory, metal, etc" includes furniture such as tables that often contain very small percentages of ivory, if any at

Table 3.8: India's imports by commodity/country

Article Code	Articles Countries Units of Quantity	April 1985 to March 1986 Quantity (kg)	Value (Rs)
8960708	Ivory manf n.e.s.** as artware		
	Hong Kong		254,982
			254,982*
8991103	Ivory workd and artcls therof		
	Denmark	166	60,253
	German F Rep	14	29,580
		182*	89,833*
8960708	Ivory manf n.e.s. as artware		
	Australia		23,923
	Belgium		106,498
	Bulgaria		1,297
	Canada	171,875	377,175
	Denmark	38,250	406,891
	France	297,509	855,250
	German F Rep		912,694
	Hong Kong	24,160	72,474
	Italy	266,908	385,328
	Japan		234,448
	Kuwait		12,000
	Netherland	29,170	32,897
	Norway		17,000
	Quatar		238,514
	Saudi Arabia		46,400
	Spain	60,050	146,362
	Switzerland		19,400
	UAE		128,654
	UK	22,636	78,697
	USA	425,472	6,053,137
		1,336,030*	10,149,035*

Note: * indicates total
   ** not elsewhere specified

all, and again the value of objects will vary tremendously. Generally, this last category is not included in worked ivory statistics as the volume of ivory is highly ambiguous and is likely to be very small.

Classification is not standard across countries. In other situations, worked ivory may be classed along with a range of other articles of other composition, for example, of horn, hair, hoof, etc. (see p. 52). The category is unlikely to give a breakdown of the individual items imported/exported and no indication of the percentage of the imports/exports from ivory. Aggregating such data to obtain an indication of the total level of imports and exports of a country over time may not be possible as the categories are incompatible. What is more, comparison of aggregate volumes and values between individual countries is likely to be extremely difficult and often unreliable.

If Hong Kong records exports of worked ivory to France, one would expect France in turn to record the same value and volume of imports from Hong Kong. However, there are a variety of incentives to misinform and to avoid trade regulations. Thus, even where data are available, they are often unreliable. For example, in order to avoid regulations imposed on raw ivory trading, ivory was often simply cut or semi-carved before it was traded. This was then traded as worked ivory. Worked ivory data does not indicate the degree of manufacture.

It is recommended that future records of worked ivory should be made more comprehensive. A common stance on the categorization of worked ivory would greatly help in determining trade flows and transactions. It would be helpful if the data collected were more explicit – recording both weight and value, listing what the items are, the percentage weight of ivory in the items, and whether the ivory is at intermediate or final stages of working.

Notes

1. Much of the data for this chapter are based upon the "Worked Ivory Trade Database" compiled by Emma Penfold for the London Environmental Economics Centre for the Ivory Trade Review Group, 1989. We wish to express our thanks to her for all her hard work.
2. "The Ivory Crisis", *Asiaweek*, (5 August 1988), pp 20–39.
3. According to Hong Kong customs statistics, during the period 1979–88, raw ivory imports, including scrap, into Hong Kong amounted to 3,970,581kg. CITES data record a slightly lower figure of 3,948,179kg. See T. Milliken and D. Melville, "The Hong Kong Ivory Trade", draft

report to the Second Meeting of the CITES African Elephant Working Group, Gabarone, Botswana (July 1989). Much of the following data is based upon statistics appendixed to this Report.

4. Milliken and Melville, op. cit. (Note 3).

5. E.B. Martin, *The Japanese Ivory Industry* (WWF: Japan, 1985).

6. This is examined in more detail in two papers prepared by E.B. Barbier, "The Demand for Unworked Ivory: A Case Study of Japan", Economics Working Paper ITRG/EG 89-01, (February 1989), and "The Demand for Unworked Ivory: A Case Study of Hong Kong", Economics Working Paper ITRG/EG 89-09, (April 1989). Both papers were prepared as part of the LEEC contribution to the ITRG report, *The Ivory Trade and the Future of the African Elephant*, prepared for the Second Meeting of the CITES African Elephant Working Group, Gabarone, Botswana (July, 1989). The analysis is published in E.B. Barbier and J.C. Burgess, *The Demand for African Elephant Ivory*, LEEC Discussion Papers, (IIED: London, 1989).

7. Milliken and Melville, op. cit. (Note 3).

8. T. Milliken, "Japan's Ivory Trade" in *Traffic Bulletin*, vol. 7 (3/4) (1985), p. 43.

9. The following information is based on data from the Japan country study by T. Milliken, Chapter VI.7 "The Japanese Ivory Trade: Tradition, CITES and the Elusive Search for Sustainable Utilisation", in the ITRG Report *The Ivory Trade and the Future of the African Elephant*, (See Note 6 for details.)

10. For details of the uses of ivory in Japan see T. Milliken, op. cit. (Note 9).

11. Milliken, op. cit. (Note 9).

12. Martin, op. cit. (Note 5).

13. See Chapter 5, by D.W. Pearce, "The Final Demand for Raw Ivory", prepared as the LEEC contribution in the ITRG report, *The Ivory Trade and the Future of the African Elephant*. (See Note 6 for details).

14. See Chapter VI.1 by R. Luxmoore, J. Caldwell and L. Hithersay, "The UK Ivory Trade", in the ITRG Report, *The Ivory Trade and the Future of the African Elephant*. (See Note 6 for details.)

15. Worked ivory statistics for most of the European countries and the USA were collected and compiled by the LEEC as a "Worked Ivory Trade Database" for ITRG, 1989 (see Note 1).

16. I.S.C. Parker, *The Ivory Trade*, (US Fish and Wildlife Service: Washington DC, 1979).

17. See J. Thomsen, Chapter VI.5 "The Ivory Trade in the USA" in the ITRG report, *The Ivory Trade and the Future of the African Elephant*. (See Note 6 for details.)

18. The information on elephant skins is drawn heavily from J.B. Thomsen, "Recent US Imports of Certain Products from the African Elephant", *Pachyderm*, no. 10, (January 1988), pp. 1-21.

19. Thomsen, op. cit. (Note 18).

20. J. Barzdo, "The Worked Ivory Trade", *Traffic Bulletin*, vol. 6 (2), (1984), pp. 21-6.

21. J. Thomsen, "Ivory, CITES, and the US Connection", *Traffic (USA)*, 8(2), (1988), pp. 6-7.
22. Based upon the USA country study by J. Thomsen in the ITRG Report, *The Ivory Trade and the Future of the African Elephant*. (See Note 6 for details.)
23. The following information was recorded in a report on the WWF Elephant Workshop, Lusaka, Zambia, April 1988.
24. E.B. Martin, "China's Ivory Carving Industry", *Traffic Bulletin*, vol. 10(1/2), (1988), pp. 4-7.
25. Martin, op. cit. (Note 24).
26. E.B. Martin, (1980). "The Craft, the Trade and the Elephants", *Oryx*, 15(4), (1980), pp. 363-6.
27. E.B. Martin, *The Japanese Ivory Industry*, (WWF: Japan, 1985).
28. Martin, op. cit. (Note 27).
29. See Chapter VI.10 by A. Laurie, "The Ivory Trade in Guangzhou, China" in the ITRG Report, *The Ivory Trade and the Future of the African Elephant*. (See Note 6 for details.)
30. For further details of India's role in the ivory trade see Martin, op. cit. (Note 26).
31. A recent update and expansion of the previous E.B. Martin report (1980) (op. cit. Note 26) is provided in E.B. Martin and L. Vigne, "The Decline and Fall of India's Ivory Industry", in *Pachyderm*, no. 12, (1989), pp. 4-22. Also see Chapter VI.6 by E.B. Martin and L. Vigne, "The Decline and Fall of India's Ivory Industry" in the ITRG report, *The Ivory Trade and the Future of the African Elephant*. (See Note 6 for details.)
32. Martin and Vigne, op. cit. (Note 31, first ref.).
33. Martin and Vigne, op. cit. (Note 31, first ref.).
34. Much of the following data for the newly established carving centres is taken from Milliken and Melville, op. cit. (Note 6).
35. See D.W. Pearce, Chapter 5, "The Final Demand for Raw Ivory", from the ITRG Report, *The Ivory Trade and the Future of the African Elephant*. (See Note 6 for details.)
36. *Asiaweek*, (1988), op. cit. (Note 2).
37. Ying Wang and T. Milliken, "The Ivory Trade in Taiwan", in the ITRG Report, *The Ivory Trade and the Future of the African Elephant*. (See Note 6 for details).
38. T. Milliken, "The Japanese Ivory Trade: Tradition, CITES, and the Elusive Search for Sustainable Utilisation", in the ITRG Report, *The Ivory Trade and the Future of the African Elephant*. (See Note 6 for details.)

4 DEMAND ANALYSIS: JAPAN AND HONG KONG

Introduction

This section examines the trends in total and net demand for unworked (raw) ivory of Japan and Hong Kong over the periods 1950–87 and 1962–87 respectively. The analysis is based on two econometric models:

i) a relatively simple estimation of the *income- and price-elasticities of demand* at a national level;[1] and,

ii) a more elaborate model that attempts to calculate price elasticities while also including an *asset-demand* motivation for holding ivory.[2]

The following section discusses the results of these two models; further details of the analysis can be found in two papers by Barbier, "The Demand for Unworked Ivory: A Case Study of Japan" (1989) and "The Demand for Unworked Ivory: A Case Study of Hong Kong" (1989).[3] This analysis is important for determining appropriate policies for controlling the ivory trade.

Clearly, one key to regulating the world trade in ivory lies in controlling the demand by end-use consuming countries. To a large extent, this policy option appears to have been foreclosed by the recent decision, in October 1989, by CITES to impose an indefinite trade ban on all ivory products. Japan has accepted this ban, which it put into operation on 1 November 1989. At the time of writing (March 1990), Hong Kong's position has not been officially confirmed. However, the current agreement carries an amendment allowing a limited trade by those African producer countries which are able to demonstrate an ability to manage their elephant populations sustainably. There is also concern that the ban will not stop, but may even incite, further illegal trade in elephant ivory.[4] And, as noted, several southern African states have opted for reservations from the CITES ban, and will be continuing to trade. Controlling the end-use demand for ivory by consuming nations will therefore be relevant in any future strategy considerations.

The tax option

One option that should be explored is whether consumer countries such as Japan and Hong Kong should employ a tax to reduce end-use demand. A tax would raise the price of ivory in the importing country, thus reducing demand. An analysis of the relationships between demand, real ivory prices and income in such countries is needed to evaluate this option.

Japan is a major consumer of raw ivory (see "Japan Analysis", p. 83). Calculating the income- and price-elasticities of demand in Japan is important for designing appropriate policies to limit demand, and thus controlling the global trade in raw ivory. There are at least four policy-relevant features of empirical estimates of demand elasticity. First, a low *price*-elasticity of demand would suggest that a tax on raw ivory imports would not be effective in significantly reducing end-use demand. Second, the asset-demand model should also indicate the extent to which unworked ivory is held as a store of value. Since interest rates cannot be influenced by specific policies aimed at the ivory trade, a high *interest*-elasticity may limit the extent to which demand-control or supply-control policies will influence trade. Third, if demand is price-inelastic there are implications for the gains that would be made if producers – i.e. countries of export origin – cooperated to restrict the supply of ivory. Fourth, the measure of *income*-elasticity will show how sensitive ivory demand will be to economic growth in final consuming countries, and will thus enable a better idea to be obtained of how elephant population decline might be projected into the future.

Hong Kong also is a major importer of raw ivory. Calculating the income- and price-elasticities of demand by Hong Kong is important for designing appropriate policies to limit demand, and thus controlling the global trade in ivory. However, unlike Japan, Hong Kong is less of a final source of end-use demand than a major entrepôt in the world ivory trade. A significant proportion of its imports of raw ivory are re-exported to other countries. The resulting net imports may be held as stockpiled inventories, to be exported later, or used as raw materials for its carving industry, which may also be eventually exported as worked ivory. Thus, net imports do not necessarily indicate final end-use consumption of ivory in Hong Kong.

Nevertheless, in order to determine whether any policy interventions are feasible at this entrepôt stage in the world ivory trade, it is important to analyse the elasticities of demand and asset-demand motivation for importing ivory in trading countries such as Hong Kong. For example, a high price-elasticity of demand would suggest that a tax on raw ivory imports into entrepôt countries might be effective in controlling the world trade. The analysis should cover both gross imports, which include re-exported ivory, and net imports. At the very least, this should reveal whether policy interventions are more effective at the final end-use demand stage of the ivory trade rather than at the entrepôt stage as represented by Hong Kong.

Japan Analysis

Background

Japan's end-use demand, or final consumption, of raw ivory remained fairly stable in the 1950s and early 1960s, but then increased dramatically from the late 1960s to the early 1980s (Figure 4.1 and Table 4.1).[5] For example, at its peak in 1983 raw ivory consumption was 15 times its level in 1950.

In the early 1980s, the relative importance of Hong Kong as the centre of the ivory trade was overtaken by Japan. A major reason cited is that, although in 1980 Japan accepted the control of imported tusks agreed under CITES, up to 1985 Hong Kong's legislation has

---

Figure 4.1: Japan: consumption of raw ivory, 1950–87

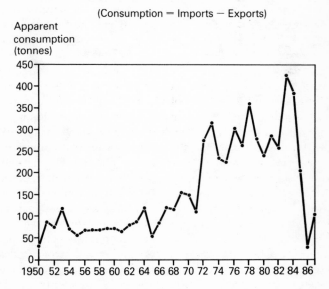

Source: London Environmental Economics Centre.

Table 4.1: Japan: imports of raw ivory, 1950–87

	(kg)		*(US$)*	*(US$/kg)*	*(JY/US$)*	*(JY)*	*(JY/kg)*
1950	28,725		82,597.29	2.88	360.00	29,735,024.4	1,035.16
1951	86,573		350,793.50	4.05	360.00	126,285,660.0	1,458.72
1952	72,425		267,052.94	3.69	360.00	96,139,058.4	1,327.43
1953	118,492		454,046.21	3.83	360.00	163,456,635.6	1,379.47
1954	69,280		379,419.44	5.48	360.00	136,590,998.4	1,971.58
1955	55,788		332,019.44	5.95	360.00	119,526,998.4	2,142.52
1956	66,618		392,577.78	5.89	360.00	141,328,000.8	2,121.47
1957	67,343		417,761.11	6.20	360.00	150,393,999.6	2,233.25
1958	67,329		411,727.76	6.12	360.00	148,221,993.6	2,201.46
1959	71,171		441,844.44	6.21	360.00	159,063,998.4	2,234.96
1960	70,986		458,566.64	6.46	360.00	165,083,990.4	2,325.59
1961	64,511		398,983.33	6.18	360.00	143,633,998.8	2,226.50
1962	79,378		461,399.99	5.81	360.00	166,103,996.4	2,092.57
1963	86,086		483,919.43	5.62	360.00	174,210,994.8	2,023.69
1964	120,319		668,519.44	5.56	360.00	240,666,998.4	2,000.24
1965	52,497		354,305.53	6.75	360.00	127,549,990.8	2,429.66
1966	83,259		642,924.98	7.72	360.00	231,452,992.8	2,779.92
1967	120,143		841,866.66	7.01	360.00	303,071,997.6	2,522.59
1968	115,341		791,399.98	6.86	360.00	284,903,992.8	2,470.10
1969	155,520		1,013,969.43	6.52	360.00	365,028,994.8	2,347.15
1970	149,415	a/	1,567,999.98	10.49	360.00	564,479,992.8	3,777.93
1970	141,411	b/	1,459,955.54	10.32	360.00	525,583,994.4	3,716.71
1971	110,241	a/	1,787,774.95	16.22	349.33	624,523,423.3	5,665.07
1971	100,738	b/	1,719,105.79	17.07	349.33	600,535,225.6	5,961.36
1972	275,497	a/	5,452,745.08	19.79	303.17	1,653,108,725.9	6,000.46
1972	274,657	b/	5,439,799.51	19.81	303.17	1,649,184,017.4	6,004.52
1973	315,640		15,521,003.34	49.17	271.70	4,217,056,607.5	13,360.34
1974	233,716		10,994,649.76	47.04	292.08	3,211,317,301.9	13,740.24
1975	223,793		11,066,089.35	49.45	296.79	3,284,304,658.2	14,675.64
1976	306,786	a/	11,266,717.08	36.73	296.47	3,340,266,026.9	10,887.93
1976	303,759	b/	11,225,957.88	36.96	296.47	3,328,188,959.3	10,956.65
1977	266,888	a/	10,501,471.13	39.35	267.38	2,807,880,074.4	10,520,81
1977	262,967	b/	10,436,619.57	39.69	267.38	2,790,540,062.3	10,611.75
1978	368,377	a/	26,305,147.33	71.41	208.33	5,480,238,150.8	14,876.71
1978	359,192	b/	26,148,551.89	72.80	208.33	5,447,614,105.0	15,166.30
1979	296,864	a/	24,867,378.78	83.77	219.88	5,467,672,025.9	18,418.10
1979	279,288	b/	24,490,309.20	87.69	219.88	5,384,734,083.4	19,280.22
1980	274,019	a/	20,911,277.71	76.31	225.84	4,722,516,061.0	17,234.26
1980	239,981	b/	20,218,371.89	84.25	225.84	4,566,027,945.1	19,026.62
1981	308,231	a/	24,381,025.25	79.10	220.26	5,364,362,012.3	17,403.770
1981	286,070	b/	23,931,956.52	83.66	220.26	5,263,556,895.3	18,406.53
1982	284,846	a/	21,744,843.70	76.34	248.26	5,398,421,865.1	18,952.07
1982	257,419	b/	21,078,801.92	81.89	248.26	5,233,068,895.5	20,328.99
1983	475,666	a/	29,934,654.57	62.93	237.42	7,106,992,890.7	14,941.14
1983	424,950	b/	28,565,615.37	67.22	237.42	6,781,959,847.5	15,959.43
1984	473,782	a/	31,995,887.59	67.53	237.25	7,590,957,779.0	16,022.04
1984	384,442	b/	29,002,407.51	75.44	237.25	6,880,760,856.8	17,898.04
1985	286,529	a/	24,356,120.57	85.00	236.74	5,766,126,925.9	20,124.06
1985	206,004	b/	20,487,363.13	99.45	236.74	4,850,227,927.6	23,544.33
1986	79,122	a/	9,176,519.71	115.98	167.48	1,536,848,008.4	19,423.77
1986	28,840	b/	6,566,475.78	227.69	167.48	1,099,727,950.7	38,132.03
1987	142,984	a/	21,553,042.12	150.74	144.66	3,117,665,030.3	21,804.29
1987	103,261	b/	19,092,495.26	184.90	144.66	2,761,744,977.6	26,745.28

Notes: a/ Total imports.

　　　　b/ Net imports (apparent consumption) = imports less exports.

　　　　N.B. Imports under CCCN category 509.600 excluded for 1984–87.

Source: London Environmental Economics Centre.

been more effective than Japan's in implementing CITES rules for raw ivory. As a result, illegitimate suppliers of ivory from Africa reduced their exports to Hong Kong, which subsequently became more reliant upon Japan as a source of supply.[6] Thus, in the 1980s, re-exports to Hong Kong initially began absorbing a growing proportion of Japan's gross imports of raw ivory, but since 1984 the trade has experienced a steady decline back to pre-1983 levels (Table 4.1).

However, in 1985 Japan introduced an amendment to the Import Trade Control Order which implements the "Japan Laws, Ordinances and Other Regulations Concerning Foreign Exchange and Foreign Trade". This amendment eliminated the acceptability of country of origin certificates, and required the presentation of valid CITES permits from the country of export or re-export. At the same time, the ivory importers self-imposed a further measure, namely, to present all documents covering individual shipments to the CITES Secretariat for review before importation into Japan is allowed. If any discrepancies are noted, the Japanese dealers reject the transaction. Therefore, Japanese ivory transactions have been "transparent" (i.e. the tremendous volumes of ivory moving outside CITES channels have become more visible) and subject to constant examination since 1985.[7]

The new regulation began affecting raw ivory imports in the second half of 1985, and in 1986 gross imports fell to their lowest level in 20 years (Table 4.1). Thus, since its peak in 1983, Japan's consumption of raw ivory has fallen rapidly and although there was a slight recovery in 1987, the 1988 figure will be less than 100 tonnes, approximately 40 tonnes less than the 1987 trade. This is further evidence that imports of raw ivory to Japan remain substantially reduced (Figure 4.1).

Given that Japan is a major end-use consumer of ivory, the main effect of the 1985 Japanese regulation has been to create a block at the importing end of the illegal trade route. This may have given rise to the diversion of illegal ivory to entrepôts and importing consumers that have a less strict control on exports. An example of this is the subsequent large-scale stockpiling of illegal ivory in Macau, Singapore, and Dubai, destinations which largely rose and fell in the sequential order noted (Tom Milliken, pers. comm.).[8] When Japanese regulations took effect, the illegal traffic from Africa became more transparent. It remains to be documented to what extent, if at all, this trade represents an increase over previous years.

Demand analysis
In Japan, real raw ivory prices – the per unit value of net imports of

Figure 4.2: Japan: real raw ivory prices, 1950–87 (at 1980 prices)

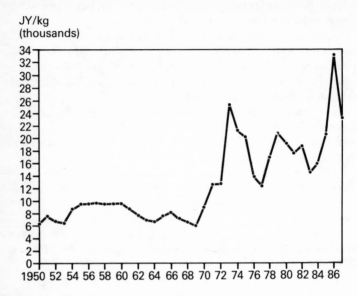

Source: London Environmental Economics Centre.

raw ivory deflated by the consumer price index – were significantly higher, but more volatile, in the 1970s and 1980s compared to the 1950s and 1960s (Figure 4.2). Over the period 1983–6, Japanese real raw ivory prices rose sharply but then fell back in 1987, which may have contributed significantly to the trends in final consumption over 1983–7 discussed above. This suggests that, in recent years at least, Japanese consumption of raw ivory is sensitive to changes in its real price. Another view put forward is that this could have been an artefact of better control: that is, the imposition of trade controls have cut off the supply of illegal ivory, and driven the demanded price of legal ivory higher, and as a consequence the price of imported ivory has risen.

Returning to Table 4.1, over the 1970–87 period for which data are available, the per unit value of Japanese net imports of raw ivory tends generally to exceed that of gross imports. This would suggest that Japanese re-exports of raw ivory tend to be of lower value than raw ivory retained for domestic consumption. This may be accounted for by Hong Kong tending to import smaller and inferior quality tusks than Japan. Ivory might therefore be a luxury consumption good in Japan, which may make it more amenable to control by taxation. Both the income- and price-elasticities of demand for raw ivory should therefore be analysed.

There is also a need to analyse whether investors are attracted to ivory as a store of wealth, especially in times of high inflation. For example, at the global level, the real value of ivory was six times higher in 1978 than in 1960, and at no time since 1973 has the real value been less than three times its average for the 1960s.[9] If there is a significant asset-demand for ivory in consuming and entrepôt countries, then the returns to holding it should be greater than those obtained from an alternative asset. A proxy for the latter would be the real rate of interest in the importing country. Figure 4.3 compares for Japan the percentage change in real raw ivory prices to the real interest rate (both at 1980 prices). The real interest rate has fallen

Figure 4.3: Japan: percentage change in real raw ivory prices and real discount rates, 1951–87 (at 1980 prices)

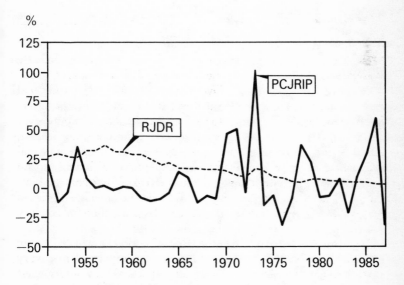

Source: London Environmental Economics Centre.

Table 4.2: Summary of elasticities of demand for raw ivory by Japan

	MODEL I No interest rate variable, net imports	MODEL 2 With interest rate variable, net imports	
		With constant	Without constant
PRICE ELASTICITY			
i) current yr	–0.52	–0.70	–0.72
INCOME ELASTICITY			
i) current yr	+1.00	+1.15	+1.53
INTEREST ELASTICITY			
i) current yr	na	+0.34	+0.37
ii) lagged 1 yr	na	–0.40	–0.26

Source: E.B. Barbier, "The Demand for Unworked Ivory: A Case Study of Japan", Economics Working Paper ITRG/EG 89-01, (February 1989)

steadily since 1950, whereas the percentage change in real raw ivory prices has fluctuated significantly, particularly since 1970. If an asset-demand for raw ivory exists, it may be cyclical; i.e. only over certain years may the capital gains from holding ivory exceed those earned from other assets.

Appendix 4.1 contains the basic model used for estimating the demand for importing raw ivory by Japan. Several versions of the model were tested.[10] The results are summarized in Table 4.2. Simple estimation of the elasticities of Japanese end-use demand for raw ivory reveals a price-elasticity of about one half and an income-elasticity of approximately unity. When an asset-demand motivation is included, price-elasticity increases to over 0.7 and income-elasticity rises to at least 1.15, and in the best model, to over 1.53. Intuitively, this seems reasonable. If ivory is being held as a store of wealth, one would expect it to be more income-elastic (i.e. more of a luxury good), and one would also expect demand to become more sensitive to changes in real prices, as these now determine the returns on ivory as an asset.

Although the above models do seem to present reasonable evidence that such an asset-demand motivation for holding ivory in Japan does exist, further work is required before one can conclusively reject the hypothesis that no such motivation is at work. Equally important, if such a relationship does exist, more analysis is required before the actual mechanics and magnitude of the asset-demand for ivory can be satisfactorily revealed.

However, the elasticities estimated from the above models do indicate a number of important policy implications. First, as the demand for raw ivory in Japan seems to be significantly sensitive to real prices as well as income-elastic, there appears to be some scope for the use of import taxes as a means of discouraging domestic consumption. For example, assuming a 0.7 price-elasticity, a domestic tax on consumption that raised real ivory prices by 10 per cent would reduce the 1987 level of consumption by 7.2 tonnes. Taxes that *doubled* the real price of raw ivory would reduce Japanese consumption by about 70 per cent, which in 1987 would have meant a total net import level after the tax of 7,228 kg – about the level of gross imports in Japan in the early 1960s (Table 4.1).

As raw ivory demand in Japan appears to be fairly income-elastic, it is essential to take measures to reduce consumption as real GNP in Japan continues to expand at around 4 per cent per annum. This could increase ivory consumption by 6.1 per cent each year – or an additional 6.3 tonnes, based on 1987 levels. In addition, the high income-elasticity of demand for ivory would suggest that any tax would be progressive. Thus one would anticipate that the higher income groups in Japan would bear proportionately more of the burden of taxation, particularly if there is a strong asset-demand motivation for holding ivory.

Imposing high taxes on raw ivory consumption in Japan would not be effective without further tightening of CITES controls and other import legislation that has a bearing on ivory imports. In particular, any possible loopholes that *may* allow in illegal ivory, or ivory imports without proper documentation if it is only slightly worked or cut, need to be closed. In turn it may also be necessary to impose taxes on all worked ivory permanently entering Japan. Moreover, a major advantage of combining taxes with existing and improved controls is to counteract any smuggling – if it exists – of raw ivory into Japan.[11] A sales or value added tax on ivory consumed within Japan would further discourage demand, whether the raw ivory was legally imported or smuggled.

The ultimate aim of taxes and regulations on net imports of raw ivory into countries that are large end-use consumers, such as Japan, is to facilitate control of the global trade and thus, it is hoped, help end the over-exploitation of elephant populations in Africa. Unfortunately, stricter controls and the use of taxes by one or even a few consuming countries may reduce their domestic consumption of raw ivory significantly, but may not necessarily affect the global legal and illegal trade if this is diverted to new entrepôts and end-use consumers who have less strict policies and controls. Already, there is evidence of such diversions taking place in response to the stronger controls imposed by Japan and recent (1988) strengthening of regulations in Hong Kong. Moreover, there is the unknown factor of how a fall in demand in Japan will affect the trading price of raw ivory. On the other hand, if Japan is successful in substantially reducing its domestic consumption of raw ivory through the combination of taxes and regulations, increased pressure through CITES and other organizations could be put on other consuming countries to follow suit. The demonstration of effective controls is preferable to *ad hoc* implementation of untried and possibly dubious controls.

Finally, a price-inelastic demand for ivory is one of the conditions favourable to the formation of an ivory producers' exporting cartel (IPEC). If the African exporters can form an IPEC and collude on price

Figure 4.4: Hong Kong: imports of raw ivory, 1952–87

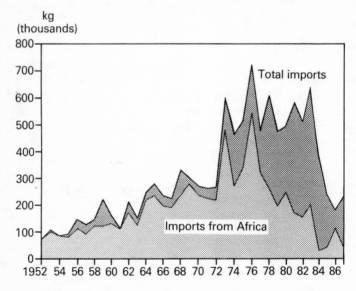

Source: London Environmental Economics Centre.

fixing and quota arrangements, the low price-elasticity of demand for Japan – a major consuming country – suggests that revenues for the cartel can be raised by restricting exports of raw ivory.

Hong Kong Analysis

Background
Hong Kong's total, or gross, imports of raw ivory increased steadily during the 1950s and 1960s, grew dramatically in the mid-1970s,

Table 4.3: Hong Kong: total imports of raw ivory, 1952–87

	(kg)	*(US$)*	*(US$/kg)*	*(HK$/US$)*	*(HK$)*	*(HK$/kg)*
1952	71,386	284,649	3.99	5.71	1,626,484	22.78
1953	107,880	482,061	4.47	5.71	2,754,497	25.53
1954	86,440	372,815	4.31	5.71	2,130,265	24.64
1955	93,211	424,536	4.55	5.71	2,425,799	26.02
1956	144,653	693,573	4.79	5.71	3,963,076	27.40
1957	126,151	620,165	4.92	5.71	3,343,623	28.09
1958	145,058	750,501	5.17	5.71	4,288,363	29.56
1959	220,626	915,231	4.15	5.71	5,229,630	23.70
1960	157,751	874,926	5.55	5.71	4,999,327	31.69
1961	115,112	598,501	5.20	5.71	3,419,835	29.71
1962	212,804	1,091,675	5.13	5.71	6,237,831	29.31
1963	148,544	808,217	5.40	5.71	4,618,152	30.88
1964	243,639	1,373,105	5.64	5.71	7,845,922	32.20
1965	276,400	1,885,366	6.82	5.71	10,772,981	38.98
1966	234,596	1,473,326	6.28	5.71	8,418,585	35.89
1967	223,017	1,205,727	5.41	6.06	7,307,911	32.77
1968	329,928	1,698,156	5.15	6.06	10,292,524	31.20
1969	299,111	1,642,851	5.49	6.06	9,957,320	33.29
1970	267,444	2,095,489	7.84	5.71	11,954,765	44.70
1971	260,006	2,394,653	9.21	5.70	13,649,522	52.50
1972	261,509	2,624,065	10.03	5.09	13,356,491	51.07
1973	597,122	15,159,797	25.39	4.93	74,737,799	125.16
1974	464,838	12,608,964	27.13	4.93	62,162,193	133.73
1975	512,986	14,521,454	28.31	5.04	73,188,128	142.67
1976	720,631	18,405,349	25.54	4.88	89,782,192	124.59
1977	477,197	14,020,306	29.38	4.65	65,210,729	136.65
1978	610,864	32,243,732	52.78	4.67	150,671,647	246.65
1979	474,208	26,797,404	56.51	5.00	133,987,023	282.55
1980	494,271	26,929,475	54.48	4.98	133,977,491	271.06
1981	577,204	23,865,390	41.35	5.62	134,075,228	232.28
1982	510,626	21,089,352	41.30	6.06	127,814,255	250.31
1983	638,292	24,600,911	38.54	7.25	178,267,475	279.29
1984	381,927	18,535,158	48.53	7.82	144,906,679	379.41
1985	238,958	13,487,189	56.44	7.79	105,074,784	439.72
1986	181,522	11,167,177	61.52	7.79	87,000,241	479.28
1987	225,370	16,717,374	74.18	7.79	130,240,221	577.90

N.B. Values reported by customs for Singapore adjusted one decimal place over 1977–83.
Source: London Environmental Economics Centre.

sustained these high levels in the early 1980s and then declined sharply after 1983 (Figure 4.4 and Table 4.3). The level of annual imports over 1985-7 – approximately 200 tonnes – is roughly the same as import levels in the early 1960s.

Trends in net imports have largely followed those of gross imports (Figure 4.4 and Table 4.4). The share of Hong Kong's re-exports of raw ivory in total imports by weight was roughly 20–25 per cent in the early 1960s, dipped to under 20 per cent in the late 1960s and early

Table 4.4: Hong Kong: net imports of raw ivory, 1952–87

	(kg)	*(US$)*	*(US$/kg)*	*(HK$/US$)*	*(HK$)*	*(HK$/kg)*
1952	71,386	284,649	3.99	5.71	1,626,484	22.78
1953	107,880	482,061	4.47	5.71	2,754,497	25.53
1954	86,440	372,815	4.31	5.71	2,130,265	24.64
1955	93,211	424,536	4.55	5.71	2,425,799	26.02
1956	144,653	693,573	4.79	5.71	3,963,076	27.40
1957	126,151	620,165	4.92	5.71	3,543,623	28.09
1958	145,058	750,501	5.17	5.71	4,288,363	29.56
1959	220,626	915,231	4.15	5.71	5,229,630	23.70
1960	157,751	874,926	5.55	5.71	4,999,327	31.69
1961	115,112	598,501	5.20	5.71	3,419,835	29.71
1962	174,856	847,120	4.84	5.71	4,840,445	27.68
1963	113,409	576,087	5.08	5.71	3,291,759	29.03
1964	167,197	854,745	5.11	5.71	4,884,014	29.21
1965	208,009	1,393,897	6.70	5.71	7,964,729	38.29
1966	173,363	1,078,989	6.22	5.71	6,165,345	35.56
1967	190,526	963,748	5.06	6.06	5,841,276	30.66
1968	275,844	1,309,332	4.75	6.06	7,935,862	28.77
1969	262,033	1,390,519	5.31	6.06	8,427,933	32.16
1970	234,772	1,750,340	7.46	5.71	9,985,690	42.53
1971	213,118	1,737,128	8.15	5.70	9,901,630	46.46
1972	197,290	1,492,424	7.56	5.09	7,596,438	38.50
1973	339,365	5,751,132	16.95	4.93	28,353,081	83.55
1974	213,899	918,767	4.30	4.93	4,529,521	21.18
1975	372,363	8,110,191	21.78	5.04	40,875,363	109.77
1976	492,812	6,231,505	12.64	4.88	30,397,586	61.68
1977	346,504	8,571,942	24.74	4.65	39,869,497	115.06
1978	424,289	19,361,171	45.63	4.67	90,472,763	213.23
1979	366,025	17,706,453	48.37	5.00	88,532,264	241.87
1980	376,164	18,365,069	48.82	4.98	91,368,504	242.90
1981	427,336	12,890,937	30.17	5.62	72,420,995	169.47
1982	322,194	8,570,200	26.60	6.06	51,940,605	161.21
1983	442,763	12,363,000	27.92	7.25	89,586,957	202.34
1984	270,287	12,028,684	44.50	7.82	94,039,477	347.92
1985	109,373	3,534,569	32.32	7.79	27,536,805	251.77
1986	129,163	6,651,418	51.50	7.79	51,819,274	401.19
1987	150,414	7,900,399	52.52	7.79	61,549,723	409.20

Note: a/ Net imports (apparent consumption) = imports less exports.
N.B. Values reported by customs for Singapore adjusted one decimal place over 1977–83 for imports, and 1976–83 for exports.
Source: London Environmental Economics Centre.

Table 4.5: Hong Kong: share of total imports of raw ivory, 1962–87 (in percentages)

	Re-exports (%)		Net imports (%)	
	(kg)	*(HK$)*	*(kg)*	*(HK$)*
1962	17.83	22.40	82.17	77.60
1963	24.16	28.72	75.84	71.28
1964	31.38	37.75	68.62	62.25
1965	24.74	26.07	75.26	73.93
1966	26.10	26.77	73.90	73.23
1967	14.57	20.07	85.43	79.93
1968	16.39	22.90	83.61	77.10
1969	12.40	15.36	87.60	84.64
1970	12.22	16.47	87.78	83.53
1971	18.03	27.46	81.97	72.54
1972	24.56	43.13	75.44	56.87
1973	43.27	62.06	56.83	37.94
1974	53.98	92.71	46.02	7.29
1975	27.41	44.15	72.59	55.85
1976	31.61	66.14	68.39	33.86
1977	27.39	38.86	72.61	61.14
1978	30.54	39.95	69.46	60.05
1979	22.81	33.92	77.19	66.08
1980	23.90	31.80	76.10	68.20
1981	25.96	45.98	74.04	54.02
1982	36.90	59.36	63.10	40.64
1983	30.63	49.75	69.37	50.25
1984	29.23	35.10	70.77	64.90
1985	54.23	73.79	45.77	26.21
1986	28.84	40.44	71.16	59.56
1987	33.26	52.74	66.74	47.26

Source: London Environmental Economics Centre.

1970s, and, with the exception of unusually strong performances in 1973–4 and 1985, has remained at roughly 25–30 per cent ever since (Figure 4.4 and Table 4.5).

In recent years, the pattern of Hong Kong's trade in raw ivory has undergone some important changes. In the early 1980s, the relative importance of Hong Kong as the centre of the ivory trade was overtaken by Japan. A major reason cited is that up to 1985 Hong Kong has been more effective than Japan in implementing legislation agreed under CITES.[12] Two results have emerged.

First, since 1984, total imports of raw ivory into Hong Kong have fallen off dramatically (Figure 4.4 and Table 4.3). It is too early to tell whether this represents a success for CITES in permanently reducing the flow of ivory through Hong Kong, or whether the trade is temporarily adjusting – diverting ivory to the illegal trade or to entrepôts and importing countries that have less strict controls than Hong Kong and now Japan.[13] In addition, a significant trade between Japan and Hong Kong in cut and simply-worked ivory has emerged, which appears to be exploiting a loophole in CITES regulations.[14]

Second, legitimate suppliers of ivory from Africa have reduced

---

Table 4.6: Hong Kong: imports of raw ivory from Africa, 1952–87

	(kg)	*(US$)*	*(US$/kg)*	*(HK$/US$)*	*(HK$)*	*(HK$/kg)*
1952	69,990	278,279	3.98	5.71	1,590,086	22.72
1953	101,007	446,648	4.42	5.71	2,552,147	25.27
1954	83,162	357,743	4.30	5.71	2,044,144	24.58
1955	79,918	360,440	4.51	5.71	2,059,554	25.77
1956	112,927	536,685	4.75	5.71	3,066,618	27.16
1957	93,476	440,711	4.71	5.71	2,518,223	26.94
1958	121,210	618,785	5.11	5.71	3,535,737	29.17
1959	121,301	578,023	4.76	5.71	3,302,823	27.23
1960	129,331	705,421	5.45	5.71	4,030,776	31.17
1961	108,531	562,588	5.18	5.71	3,214,628	29.62
1962	170,410	868,258	5.10	5.71	4,961,226	29.11
1963	122,823	662,153	5.39	5.71	3,783,542	30.80
1964	218,197	1,226,979	5.62	5.71	7,010,958	32.13
1965	232,684	1,585,142	6.81	5.71	9,057,501	38.93
1966	195,208	1,223,837	6.27	5.71	6,993,005	35.82
1967	189,349	986,612	5.21	6.06	5,979,855	31.58
1968	232,010	1,129,556	4.87	6.06	6,846,239	29.51
1969	275,346	1,502,299	5.46	6.06	9,105,434	33.07
1970	236,151	1,833,895	7.76	5.71	10,462,371	44.30
1971	223,943	2,038,490	9.10	5.70	11,619,393	51.89
1972	216,384	2,141,461	9.90	5.09	10,900,036	50.37
1973	476,604	11,885,008	24.94	4.93	58,593,089	122.94
1974	269,078	6,571,308	24.42	4.93	32,396,548	120.40
1975	339,432	7,527,609	22.17	5.04	37,939,149	111.77
1976	543,955	14,470,163	26.60	4.88	70,586,160	129.80
1977	320,951	9,180,524	28.60	4.65	42,700,112	133.00
1978	260,817	12,483,700	47.90	4.67	58,335,047	223.70
1979	194,920	10,916,313	56.00	5.00	54,581,563	280.00
1980	246,913	11,239,226	45.50	4.98	55,916,548	226.50
1981	168,130	4,114,144	24.50	5.61	23,113,169	137.50
1982	153,351	4,264,768	27.81	6.06	25,847,084	168.55
1983	199,596	5,527,681	27.69	7.25	40,055,660	200.68
1984	29,170	1,466,446	50.27	7.82	11,464,577	393.03
1985	41,679	2,011,143	48.20	7.79	15,688,231	375.90
1986	110,714	7,429,193	67.10	7.79	57,878,687	522.78
1987	42,163	3,280,966	77.80	7.79	25,561,056	606.20

Source: London Environmental Economics Centre.

Figure 4.5: Hong Kong: real raw ivory prices, 1962–87 (at 1979–80 prices)

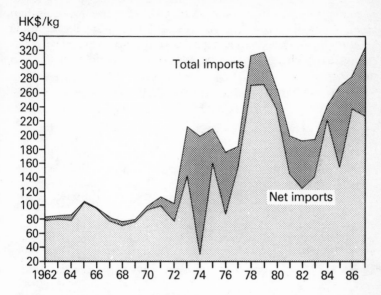

Source: London Environmental Economics Centre.

their exports to Hong Kong, which has subsequently become more reliant on Japan and other non-African suppliers. Thus the long-term trend of Hong Kong importing less ivory direct from African suppliers and increasingly from the rest of the world – in particular, Japan – seems to have accelerated in the 1980s (Table 4.6 and Figure 4.5).

Demand analysis
An important policy option that needs to be explored is whether the key to regulating the world trade in raw ivory lies in controlling the demand for it by entrepôt countries such as Hong Kong. In the case of Hong Kong, this demand consists not only of end-use domestic consumption – which may actually be quite small – but also of supplying its re-export trade and its export-oriented carving industry, as well any stockpiling that is required to service both. The demand for ivory in Hong Kong and other entrepôt countries therefore differs significantly from that in mainly end-use consuming countries, such

as Japan. Analysis of the entrepôt demand for ivory should reveal these differences.

Such an analysis should also reveal whether it is feasible for entrepôt countries such as Hong Kong to employ a tax, either on gross or net imports, to reduce their demand for ivory. (Net imports are total imports adjusted for any re-exports of raw ivory that year.) In Hong Kong, real raw ivory prices – the per unit value of total imports of raw ivory deflated by the consumer price index – rose sharply in the early 1970s and again in the late 1970s, but fell in the early 1980s before returning recently to maximum levels. Prices for net imports have generally followed similar trends (Figure 4.6). With the exception of the 1983–7 period, it is not apparent that raw ivory imports are immediately responsive to changes in real prices, although some evidence for a lagged impact seems present (Figures 4.4 and 4.6). The latter would be consistent with stockpiling of ivory.

The analysis of Japan's end-use demand for ivory indicated that the per unit value of Japanese net imports of raw ivory tends generally

Figure 4.6: Hong Kong: change in real ivory prices, 1963–87

Source: London Environmental Economics Centre.

to exceed that of gross imports (see "Japan Analysis", p. 83). This is consistent with a final consuming country that re-exports lower value raw ivory, retaining the higher valued ivory for domestic consumption. As Japan is now a major supplier of raw ivory to Hong Kong, presumably these exports are being used in the Hong Kong carving industry – perhaps to be re-exported to Japan as worked ivory. In contrast, in Hong Kong, over the period 1962–87 for which re-export data are available, the per unit value of total imports of raw ivory tends to exceed that of net imports (Tables 4.3 and 4.4). Thus, with a substantial re-export market in raw ivory and an export-oriented carving industry, Hong Kong appears to be exporting higher valued raw ivory and retaining the rest as raw material for its carvers. This again suggests that the responsiveness of both gross and net imports to price changes might be different for an entrepôt as opposed to an end-use consumer of ivory.

The need to respond to export markets of raw ivory and to supply a domestic carving industry would call for some stockpiling of raw ivory inventories. Investors may also be further attracted to stockpiling ivory as a store of wealth, especially in times of high inflation. For example, at the global level, the real value of ivory was six times higher in 1978 than in 1960, and at no time since 1973 has the real value been less than three times its average for the 1960s.[15] Thus both the real costs of holding ivory inventories, as well as the motivation for holding ivory as a store of wealth, would be negatively affected by the level of real interest rates in the economy. Figure 4.6 compares for Hong Kong the percentage change in real raw ivory prices for net imports to the real interest rate (both at 1979/80 prices). The real interest rate has fallen steadily since 1963, whereas the changes in prices have been generally more cyclical. This would suggest that if there is any impact of real interest rates on the stockpiling of ivory, it may be cyclical. Moreover, if stockpiling, including asset demand, is a significant component of the total demand for ivory in Hong Kong, this would explain the considerable fluctuations in imports as indicated in Figure 4.4.

Appendix 4.2 contains a model for the demand for raw ivory by Hong Kong. Several versions of the model were tested for both *net imports* and *total imports* of ivory by Hong Kong.[16] The estimated elasticities are summarized in Table 4.7. The results of this analysis reveal the importance of distinguishing demand for net imports from demand for total imports. The evidence suggests that Hong Kong re-exports its higher valued raw ivory while retaining lower valued ivory. It will consequently treat re-exportable ivory as a luxury good, whereas its net imports serve mainly as a raw material for its carving

Table 4.7: Summary of elasticities of demand for raw ivory by Hong Kong

	MODEL 1 *No interest rate variable*		MODEL 2 *With interest rate variable*	
	Net imports	Gross imports	Net imports	Gross imports
PRICE ELASTICITY				
i) current price	NA	+0.42	+0.48	+0.41
ii) lagged 1 yr	−0.51	−0.55	−0.20	−0.41
iii) lagged 2 yrs	+0.35	NA	NA	NA
INCOME ELASTICITY				
i) current yr	+4.43	+1.08	+0.40	+1.54
ii) lagged 1 yr	−3.52	−0.81	NA	−1.20
iii) lagged 2 yrs	−0.86	NA	NA	NA
EXCHANGE RATE ELASTICITY				
i) current yr	+4.7	+1.12	+0.67	+2.10
ii) lagged 1 yr	−5.7	−1.41	−1.07	−4.22
iii) lagged 2 yrs	NA	−2.08	NA	NA
INTEREST ELASTICITY				
i) current yr	NA	NA	+0.49	+0.47
ii) lagged 1 yr	NA	NA	−0.55	+0.72
iii) lagged 2 yrs	NA	NA	+0.83	NA

Source: E.B. Barbier, ''The Demand for Unworked Ivory: A Case Study of Hong Kong'', Economics Working Paper ITRG/EG 89–09, (February 1989).

industry and thus are characteristically income-inelastic. This is supported by the demand analysis, which yielded an income-elasticity of around 0.4 for net imports and over 1.5 for total imports (Table 4.7).

The implication is, that as the Hong Kong economy continues to develop and grow, it will tend to expand its luxury good re-export market in raw ivory relative to its carving industry. As shown in Table 4.5 and Figure 4.4, this seems to have happened up to the mid-1980s. More recently, the effect of the CITES-inspired Hong Kong legislation, but perhaps more importantly the 1985 legislation in its main export market of Japan, appears to have dampened the Hong Kong re-export trade in raw ivory. It is too early to tell whether this will be a temporary downturn, however. Nevertheless, it does suggest that controlling and reducing the demand in final end-use countries might be an effective way of limiting the re-export markets of entrepôt countries. In the short run, Hong Kong's export-oriented carving industry might be boosted by the diversion of some of the raw ivory re-export trade to the worked ivory trade. Over the long run, however, as Hong Kong continues to develop, one would expect its carving industry to be transferred to lesser developed economies.

The complex motivation for Hong Kong's demand for raw ivory imports complicates the responsiveness of imports to changes in real prices. For total imports, higher real raw ivory prices may actually spur a booming re-export trade. It is therefore unclear as to whether a tax on gross ivory imports would reduce demand. In any case, the regression results indicate that total imports are much more responsive to changes in interest rates and exchange rates (Table 4.7). For example, despite an increase in real import prices, a rising exchange rate and falling real interest rates would cause imports to expand. For net imports, the price response is more complicated still. Once again this response appears positive in the current period. This may be due to expanding supply in the carving industry pulling in more net imports, or stockpiling of higher valued raw ivory for future re-export. As in the case with gross imports, however, the price responsiveness of net imports is overshadowed by the impacts of interest rates and the exchange rate.

The complicated response of raw ivory imports into Hong Kong to changes in real (net or gross) import prices suggests caution in the use of taxation to control imports. Although imports are more responsive to interest rates and the exchange rate, these variables cannot be used to control Hong Kong's raw ivory trade because they are essentially determined by world economic factors and overall macro-economic policy. This leaves three options in the control of Hong Kong's entrepôt ivory trade:

i)   continued tightening of Hong Kong's CITES-agreed legislation;

ii) getting Hong Kong to accept a ban on its ivory trade; and,

iii) controlling trade through Hong Kong by reducing demand by the end-use consuming countries it supplies.

As discussed, although the first option is welcomed, in the long run it may divert Hong Kong's entrepôt trade to other entrepôt countries which have not adopted or have ignored CITES regulations. The estimated income-elasticity for Hong Kong's net imports of raw ivory suggests that in the long run its carving industry might shift anyway to a lesser developed country. Certainly if Hong Kong were to ban its trade in raw and newly carved ivory, the movement of its trade to other locations would be expedited. Thus, unless all existing and potential entrepôt countries accept the recent CITES ban on ivory trade, unilateral acceptance by Hong Kong may not have that much of a long-term impact on reducing the world ivory trade.

Reducing the end-use demand for raw and newly carved ivory, as well as ivory-based products, in final consuming countries could have a dramatic impact on controlling the trade, not just through Hong Kong but through other existing and potential entrepôts. As demonstrated in the demand analysis of Japan, effective policies for controlling final consumption demand can be devised. In the long run, this could be the most effective way of controlling world trade, including reducing the incentive for other entrepôts to take up trade displaced from Hong Kong. Further analysis is required, however, of the nature of the entrepôt through Hong Kong and similar countries to understand the implications of this and even the other two options on world trade.

Conclusion

Economic analysis of the demand for raw ivory by Japan and Hong Kong demonstrates that policy interventions to reduce the demand for raw ivory are possible at the final consuming-country stage of trade, and perhaps to control entrepôt trade in raw ivory. However, reduction of demand is likely to be easiest at the end-use level of trade rather than at entrepôt level.

To obtain a more complete understanding of the responsiveness of the ivory trade to economic incentives, there is a need to supplement the demand analysis of Japan and Hong Kong by extending the work to cover other major consumers and traders of raw ivory. This involves analysing the trends over time in demand for unworked ivory of such countries as the USA, the EEC, Taiwan and China.

Finally, there is an urgent need to examine the inter-relationship between the raw and worked ivory trade. The trends in the worked ivory industry and their implications for the demand for ivory as a raw material need to be determined. As indicated in the analysis of net imports into an entrepôt such as Hong Kong, this inter-relationship is extremely significant. This would also require further analysis of the demand for worked ivory exports from Hong Kong in its main foreign markets, such as the USA. Without such an analysis, only a part of the story of the entrepôt trade in ivory can be learned, thus inhibiting our ability to choose the correct policy options for controlling the global trade in ivory and ivory products.

Appendix 4.1: The Raw Ivory Demand Model: Japan

A simple method for estimating the elasticities of demand for ivory in Japan is based on a Cobb-Douglas model relating Japanese consumption of raw ivory to real raw ivory prices and real gross national product:

$$JCRI = A * (RJRIP)^b * (RJGNP)^c, \tag{1}$$

where

JCRI = Japanese consumption of raw ivory
RJRIP = real Japanese (net) import price of raw ivory (1980 prices)
RJGNP = real Japanese gross national product (1980 prices).

Thus the coefficients b and c are the price- and income-elasticity of demand respectively. A log-linear time series regression of (1) allows direct estimation of the coefficients of elasticity, b and c.

Extending the analysis to examine an asset-demand motivation for holding raw ivory essentially involves including an additional variable in (1) to account for the returns on alternative assets:

$$JCRI = A * (RJRIP)^b * (RJGNP)^c * (RJDR)^d, \tag{2}$$

where

RJDR = real Japanese discount rates (%).[17]

Thus an estimate of d would provide the interest-elasticity of demand for raw ivory. If an asset-demand relationship exists, then one would expect d to be negative; that is, as interest rates rise it is *less* attractive to hold ivory as a store of wealth.

Appendix 4.2: The Raw Ivory Demand Model: Hong Kong

A simple method for estimating the elasticities of demand for ivory in Hong Kong is based on a Cobb-Douglas model relating imports of raw ivory to real raw ivory prices, real gross domestic product and the exchange rate (HK\$/US\$). This estimation was carried out for both total and net raw ivory imports:

$$HKRI_i = A*(RHKRIP_1)^b*(RHKGDP)^c*(HKE)^d, \ i = N, T, \quad (3)$$

where

$HKRI_1$ = Hong Kong imports of raw ivory, for net (N) and total (T) imports

$RHKRIP_1$ = real Hong Kong import prices of raw ivory (1979/80 prices), for net (N) and total (T) imports

RKGDP   = real Hong Kong gross domestic product (1979/80 prices).

HKE   = HK\$/US\$ exchange rate[18]

Thus the coefficients b, c and d are the price, income and exchange rate elasticities of demand respectively. A log-linear time series regression of (3) allows direct estimation of the coefficients of elasticity, b, c and d for both net and total imports.

The above model (3) can be extended to include an additional variable to account for the asset-demand motivation for holding raw ivory, as well as for the direct costs of stockpiling. As in the analysis of Japan, the variable chosen is real interest rates:

$$HKRI_1 = A * (RHKRIP_1)^b * (RHKGDP)^c * (HKE)^d * (RHKLR)^e, \ i = N, T, \quad (4)$$

where

    RHKLR = real Hong Kong lending rates (%).[19]

An estimate of e for net and total imports would provide the interest-elasticity of demand for raw ivory. If an asset-demand relationship exists, then one would expect e to be negative; that is, as interest rates rise it is *less* attractive to hold ivory as a store of wealth. Similarly, a rise in interest rates would increase the direct costs of stockpiling raw ivory to supply the carving industry or future re-exports.

Notes

1. The *price-elasticity* of demand indicates the responsiveness of quantity demanded to changes in price; it is the ratio of the percentage change in quantity demanded to the percentage change in price. If this ratio is significantly less than one, then demand is said to be price-*inelastic*. If it is greater than one, then demand is price-*elastic*. Similarly, the *income- and interest-elasticities* of demand measure the responsiveness of quantity demanded to changes in income and average interest rates respectively, i.e. the ratio of the percentage change in quantity demanded to percentage change in income (or average interest rates).

2. As ivory is a highly valued commodity, one reason for accumulating ivory stocks may be because it is a *store of wealth*. That is, it is a valuable *asset* which may increase in worth the longer it is held. Similar assets are gold, silver, plutonium, jewels, and so forth. Individuals may therefore choose to hold stocks of ivory in the hope that its future value may be sufficiently high to realize a *capital gain*. This is the "asset-demand" for ivory. As will be made clear below, the decision to invest money in holding a stock of ivory as an asset will be inversely related to the *interest rate*, which is the opportunity cost of the money invested in this stock.

3. Both papers were prepared as part of the LEEC contribution to the ITRG Report *The Ivory Trade and the Future of the African Elephant* (1989). The analysis is reproduced in E.B. Barbier and J.C. Burgess, *Analysing the Demand for Raw Ivory: Case Studies of Japan and Hong Kong*, LEEC Discussion Paper 89-05, (IIED: London, 1989).

4. I.S.C. Parker, "Draft Report on the Ivory Trade", a Report to CITES, (*mimeo*, 1989). R. Simmons and U. Kreuster, "Herd Mentality: Banning Ivory Sales is No Way to Save the Elephant", *Policy Review*, (Washington DC, 1989).

5. Consumption of raw ivory by Japan is equivalent to its net imports, i.e. gross imports less re-exports in the same year. Unfortunately, custom data on re-exports by Japan were only available from 1970 onwards (Table 4.1). As noted below, however, only in the 1980s have Japan's re-exports of raw ivory increased significantly (mainly to Hong Kong). Also note that for the 1984-7 period, ivory waste and powder imports have been ignored.

6. J.R. Caldwell, "Recent Developments in the Raw Ivory Trade of Hong Kong and Japan", *Traffic Bulletin*, vol. 6, no. 2 (1984), pp. 16-20. J.R. Caldwell, "The Effect of Recent Legislative Changes on the Pattern of World Trade in Raw Ivory", *Traffic Bulletin*, vol. 9, no. 1, (1987), pp. 6-10.

7. According to the TRAFFIC office in Japan.

8. Thus in recent years there has been a flourishing illegal trade, via Burundi to the United Arab Emirates, and probably on to India with the emergence of Singapore and Dubai as important entrepôts for ivory trading without CITES permits, and the emergence of Taiwan and the

resurgence of China, and possibly of India, as important destinations of the trade (Parker, 1988).

9. I. Douglas-Hamilton, "African Elephants: Population Trends and Their Causes", *Oryx*, vol. 12, no. 1, (January, 1987).

10. This is examined in more detail by E.B. Barbier, "The Demand for Unworked Ivory: A Case Study of Japan", Economics Working Paper ITRG/EG 89-01 (February 1989). This paper was published as part of the LEEC contribution to the ITRG Report *The Ivory Trade and the Future of the African Elephant*(1989). The analysis is published in E.B. Barbier and J.C. Burgess, *The Demand for African Elephant Ivory*, LEEC Discussion Papers, (IIED: London, 1989).

11. J.R. Caldwell, "The Effects of Recent Legislative Changes on the Pattern of World Trade in Raw Ivory", *Traffic Bulletin*, vol. 9, no. 1, (1987), pp 6-10.

12. J.R. Caldwell, "Recent Developments in the Raw Ivory Trade of Hong Kong and Japan", *Traffic Bulletin*, vol. 6, no. 2 (1984), pp. 16-20. Caldwell, op.cit. (Note 11).

13. See Note 8.

14. Caldwell, op. cit. (Note 11).

15. Douglas-Hamilton, op.cit (Note 9).

16. This is examined in more detail by Barbier, (1989). "The Demand for Unworked Ivory: A Case Study of Hong Kong", Economics Working Paper prepared for the Ivory Trade Review Group. The analysis is published in E.B. Barbier and J.C. Burgess, (1989). *The Demand for African Elephant Ivory*, LEEC Discussion Papers, (IIED: London, 1989).

17. A *discount rate* in this context is the generic term for the rate charged by central banks for lending to commercial banks and other financial institutions. It therefore forms the basis for the entire interest rate structure of the economy.

18. Both the nominal exchange rate and the rate deflated by the consumer price index were tried in all models.

19. The Hong Kong and Shanghai Banking Corporation's quoted best lending rate, which is one of the base rates for the entire interest rate structure of Hong Kong.

5 POLICIES FOR THE REGULATION OF THE IVORY TRADE

Introduction

The previous chapters have presented data on the ivory trade – the quantities traded, the nature of the ivory demand and the aggregate value of the ivory in commerce. These studies reveal the vast quantities of ivory in international trade over the past few decades, reaching a peak in the early 1980s with a volume in excess of 1,000 tonnes per annum. They also show that much of the new, and strongest, demand is currently based in the newly rich Asian states, recently enabled by industrialization to participate in the world ivory market.

These chapters have also alluded to the biological trends regarding the African elephant. In brief, throughout most of its range, populations of the African elephant have been declining at an alarming pace. Three population studies by Douglas-Hamilton have recorded estimates of the elephant's rate of decline, from 1,340,000 (in 1979) to 720,000 (in 1987) to 637,000 (in mid-1989).[1] A modelling exercise undertaken by the Renewable Resources Assessment Group of Imperial College, University of London, found that the recorded population declines could be "almost entirely explained by the quantities of ivory exported from Africa".[2] This study determined that a "hunting mortality rate" in excess of 3.5 per cent would result in elephant population declines. Based primarily on the quantities of ivory in trade, this study found that the hunting mortality rate was at least 3–5 per cent in southern Africa and in the forest-dwelling populations (mainly central Africa), and that this rate was at least 9–18 per cent in the other populations (mainly east Africa).

Nevertheless, it is important to emphasize at the outset that it is not necessarily the case that high commercial values or high trade levels *must* translate into reduced elephant populations; in fact, the opposite should be true. This is because the elephant populations must generate a return as compensation for the use of the resources which they themselves depend upon (e.g. park lands, park staff, staff vehicles etc.). To the extent that these returns are high, more of these resources can be made available. If the returns are very low, then few resources can be invested in elephant habitat, management and protection. In this sense, high commercial valuation of a species is simply society's expression of its willingness to pay the bill for the dedication of substantial quantities of its resources to the maintenance of that species.

In the case of elephants (and many other endangered species), the potentially constructive impact of this high valuation is not being realized. This is because the policies currently in place are not adequately channelling the valuation of elephants into investment in elephants. In the first instance this must be because the domestic management schemes are not (with a few exceptions) capable of utilizing the demand for ivory as a constructive force for the sustenance of elephant populations. One of the first purposes of state sovereignty is the allocation of primary responsibility for the effective utilization of resources; any wastefulness must at least initially be the result of the abrogation of this responsibility. Thus, one remedy for this situation is the improvement of existing management schemes by means of internal reforms. Some of the basic differences between the successful and the unsuccessful management operations will be discussed in this chapter.

A second important remedy relates to the role of the international community. This option is limited, primarily because the elephant is not a true international resource. That is, for the most part, each elephant population which exists is affiliated with a single state, unlike a true international resource such as the whales. This means that the ultimate capacity to implement many reforms resides solely within the various domestic regimes. With regard to international resources, there is a role for an international commission to take sole jurisdiction over the resource (as is the case with the International Whaling Commission). With domestic resources, final jurisdiction is already determined.

Nevertheless, effective international regulation of international trade can operate as an effective substitute for effective domestic management, for the purpose of constricting ivory flows. As discussed in Chapter 1, the international ivory trade constitutes a three-tiered industry. First, there is the required maintenance and harvesting of elephants in the range states. Second, the raw ivory is shipped for carving to the manufacturing centres (historically, Hong Kong and Japan). Third, the ivory is finally purchased for use in the consumption centres (historically, the hard currency consumers: Europe, the USA and Japan). The verifiable constriction of the flow of ivory at any one of these levels would be sufficient to reduce the flow of ivory at all the others. The ivory trade is like a pipeline running between the range states and the final consumers; the restriction of the flow at any point must reduce the flow at all points. In this way, international regulation may be applied at any point in the trade in order to constrict excess flows resulting from lax management policies.

The decision to invoke international regulation itself creates a number of new and difficult problems. Most of these are ultimately attributable to its contractual nature; that is, international regulation of domestic resources must occur through the voluntary agreement and implementation of all of the relevant independent states. For the international community to secure any rights of control whatsoever over the resources within the exclusive jurisdiction of a sovereign state, the state must be induced to agree to cede these rights to the community. The voluntary nature of international regulation generates several new problems which must be solved, in addition to the determination of the appropriate level of ivory trade constriction, if the system is to have any effect.

The first problem to be solved is the creation of incentives to generate acceptance and implementation of the scheme by *all* of the necessary parties: the producing, manufacturing (carving) and consuming states. It is not usually in the interests of those at a different stage of an industry to institute measures for the benefit of those operating at an earlier or later stage. These different parties are in a competitive relationship. For example, the range states might prefer low volumes of ivory in trade and higher prices, but the carving states might prefer higher volumes (implying the use of more labour), and the consuming states might prefer lower prices.

The second problem generated by the use of an international form of regulation is the creation of the correct incentives in the producer states, by means of actions taken elsewhere. The excessive flows of ivory out of most of the range states is symptomatic of chronic under-investment in elephants (i.e. the lack of dedication of resources to these animals) by those states. However, this does not imply that restrictions of those flows, if initiated elsewhere, will necessarily increase these investment levels. If investment levels are not substantially increased, elephant populations cannot be sustained due to the competition for scarce resources. If they are not killed for their ivory, they will be killed for the land they occupy. Any solution other than a short-term one must directly address the incentives of the range states for investment in elephant populations.

The international regulation of domestic resources is problematic. It is not enough to discern potential answers to the problems; it is also necessary to institute regulations in such a way that the relevant states have incentives to undertake the desired actions.

This chapter analyses the problems afflicting the African elephant, and addresses the question of how international cooperation can attempt to solve these problems at the various levels at which the ivory trade operates. It commences with the problems experienced at the domestic management level, and then moves to the previous attempts at international regulation. Then the question is addressed: Is it possible for international regulation to assist in the management of domestic resources? The purpose of this chapter is to place all of the various solutions proposed (e.g. bans, quotas) into a single framework in an attempt to ascertain their relative implications for the sustainability of elephant stocks in Africa.

Regulation in the Range States

The most obvious policy option is the restriction of the harvesting rate at the range-state level. This is simply to point out that the elephant is not a true open-access resource; it has only been treated as such. An open-access resource is one in which there is no institution existing which vests exclusive ownership in the resource in a particular entity. In that instance it is not usually possible to secure the right to future flows from the resource stocks, and thus there is little incentive to invest in the creation of such stocks.

This is not the case in regard to the African elephant. In every range state, legislation exists vesting exclusive title in the resource with the state or its designated agencies. There is no viable means of contesting this claim to title in international law, except in regard to the very few elephant populations which actually cross international boundaries. Thus the elephant populations are not open-access resources; unlike the resources of the sea or of space, there exist recognized institutions giving exclusive rights of access to the flow of benefits arising from existing stocks of this resource.[3]

Why then do such insufficient levels of investment in the conservation of elephant stocks occur in the range states? There are three fundamentally different answers:

i)   the optimal extinction scenario;
ii) monitoring and local ownership deficiencies; and
iii) international intervention in domestic management.

The optimal extinction scenario

First, the problem might be as indicated in Appendix 1.1, that is, the elephant might be an uncompetitive resource in the international arena. The problem of optimal extinction relates to slow-growing resources unable to generate a return to investment which justifies the maintenance of stocks. There are two reasons why this might be the case.

Elephants are a classic example of a slow-growth species. Illustrative of the species' characteristics which contribute to this growth rate are the age at first calving (about 13 years) and the inter-birth interval (about 5 years). The age–ivory production relationship defines a gradual logarithmic curve, with lower rates of growth in earlier years; it takes a male elephant approximately 6 years to generate a 1 kg tusk of ivory and a female requires about 9 years.[4] By way of summary, the flow of ivory from a well-managed standing stock (of elephant ivory) has been found to be about 10 per cent per annum with respect to the elephant population in Kruger National Park, which has been maintained at 8,000 animals for a number of years.[5] This rate of production, 10 per cent, is not negligible; however, there are many assets which could potentially exceed this rate in the international market.

Another factor which contributes to the non-competitiveness of the elephant as an asset is the costliness of its maintenance. One necessary cost of producing future flows of ivory is the foregone consumption, which is derived from abstaining from current harvests of ivory. However, this is only one cost associated with the maintenance of standing stocks of elephants, and perhaps not at all the most substantial.

The most significant category of costs in elephant production is the expenditure necessary for the enforcement of the claim to ownership. A number of studies have indicated that this cost of production is very high indeed.[6] The migratory habits of the species make it difficult to monitor. The low costs and ready availability of weapons contributes to the large number of potential poachers. The consequent riskiness of being a patroller of the stock also contributes to costliness. Together these factors make it exceedingly costly to protect the claim of ownership to future flows of revenue from the stock of elephants. Recent work demonstrates a close correlation between these expenditures and successful maintenance of elephant stocks across range states; a successful management plan must necessarily undertake an expensive operation to assert its claim to ownership.[7]

A third cost consideration with regard to all wildlife utilization is the expense of land dedicated to this use. This has been accomplished in most range states by means of the establishment of national parks and protected areas, which limit the range of uses of such lands to wildlife and tourism. This is another important opportunity cost in regard to a migratory species such as the elephant, especially in the high population growth areas of Africa.

These cost factors, together with the low growth rate of elephant stocks, are disincentives to investment in elephants; i.e. the extreme costliness of such investments plus the slow rate of return combine to discourage the dedication of resources to the use and preservation of elephants. Together they create a strong a priori case for the argument that this species is subject to the forces of economically optimal extinction.

There are three countervailing factors. First, the appropriable value of elephant stocks far exceeds the mere value of standing ivory. The aggregate value of the ivory trade has not exceeded $60 million in any given year; the appropriable value of tourism in Kenya alone exceeded $375 million in each of the past several years. The work of Gardner Brown (cited in Chapter 1) estimated that the tourism value of existing elephant stocks was around $25 million in Kenya. In addition, there are numerous other values attributable to elephant stocks: other products (hides, trophies), existence, habitat, etc. Therefore the valuation of elephant stocks solely for the purpose of ivory production is extremely narrow.

Even if ivory is the sole basis of valuation, extinction is not the necessary outcome. The studies of demand in Japan (see Chapter 4) revealed a highly inelastic demand for ivory, somewhere between .50 and 70. Inelasticity provides incentives to jointly constrict production, not to expand it. In short, the revenues available to the industry vary little with the quantities produced.

The final countervailing factor to the optimal extinction scenario is the availability of alternative monitoring institutions for the enforcement of property rights. It is evident that the least-cost method of monitoring elephants is not being utilized in most of the range states, and this is also contributing to the rapid decline in these populations; there are obvious reforms to be made to this end.

In sum, the optimal extinction scenario would suggest that it is not economically attractive to invest in the African elephant. It clearly is very costly to maintain large stocks of this relatively slow-growing resource. There are other reasons to believe, however, that this is a highly valued species, for both its products and itself. The extraordinarily high levels of demand for the various facets of the species are indicative of this valuation. This commercial value should contribute to the maintenance of stocks, not to their eradication. Then what are the alternative reasons for the observed trend of stock reductions? These reasons are best termed institutional, and deal with the owner's failure to appropriate the full measure of the species' value. These factors are considered below.

Monitoring and local ownership programmes

One means of addressing the high cost of monitoring and patrolling stocks of elephants is the delegation of this duty to local populations. This can be accomplished by means of the transference to local communities of some part of the state's rights in the animals. For example, the state might vest full title to all elephants on specified parkland with a particular tribe. Alternatively, the state might "share-crop" the elephant populations, by vesting the community with elephant rights while retaining a specified share, say 20 per cent, of the revenue flow from the community's sale of elephant products.

Such a scheme creates a well-defined ownership system and creates incentives to invest in the protection of the elephant herd. Since the objective of protecting exclusive access to the resource is implicitly transferred to the community along with the ownership rights, there no longer exists a conflict of interest between the state and the local community. That is, the state and the local community now have the same objective: protecting the stocks of elephant. This is likely to be successful for two reasons.

First, the power of hard currency is substantial in Africa, and proportionately more significant in rural areas. This is the primary factor behind the high rates of entry into the relatively risky enterprise of poaching. The means of procurement of cash in rural Africa are relatively few, and thus the attraction of ivory is magnified by this factor. To actually allow rights in elephants, in the sense of rights to future flows from existing ivory stocks, allows the legal undertaking of this enterprise; it would create incentives to protect the elephants out of the same forces of demand that now create incentives to poach them.

Second, to the extent that poaching is already undertaken by local communities, the vesting of rights serves two functions simultaneously. It creates a group of individuals with the received objective of elephant protection, while coincidently removing their principal adversaries (themselves, the former poachers) from the field.

African states which attempt to retain all wildlife rights within their departments, rather than delegating rights to communities, face three handicaps. They must find some other means of sufficiently motivating their employees to protect elephants, usually by means of increased salaries and capital investments. They must face the prospect of poaching from local communities, rather than enlisting their forces in aid of the elephants. Finally, whenever valid property rights to a resource are not vested, it is often the case that invalid ones will arise; thus, under-motivated agents of the government will secure further funds by the sale of the resource which they are intended to be protecting.

Corruption is the second factor underlying the current trend in elephant stock reductions. In the sense utilized here, corruption is simply the activity of the state's agents when they are insufficiently motivated to undertake the state's objectives. When this occurs, the agents instead utilize their power over public resources to secure gains in private markets. This is deleterious not only to the public resources, in this instance the elephant populations, but to confidence in the government in general. For these reasons, it is absolutely essential that new forms of government management of resources be implemented; the concept of local ownership of wildlife resources is a logical first step in combating corruption.

Local ownership programmes are currently in existence in Zimbabwe and in Zambia. The Communal Area Management Programmes for Indigenous Resources (CAMPFIRE) in Zimbabwe has existed since 1986 as a means of vesting local communities with rights in wildlife resources (see also p. 144). More recently, in Zambia, the Luanga Integrated Resource Development Programme has been instituted for the same purpose. Both of these programmes operate by providing local communities with a share of the revenues derived from elephant utilization, thus encouraging community involvement in management and discouraging it in poaching. There are good reasons to believe that such programmes will ultimately be very successful in reducing the aggregate costs of monitoring elephant stocks, and thus shall contribute to the preservation of viable elephant populations.[8]

International intervention in domestic management

In the vast majority of range states there has been no "legal" ivory production throughout the peak years of the ivory trade. Without exception, the legal ownership of elephant populations is vested in the state. In all but two states there have been no significant state-authorized cullings of elephant herds during this period. Thus, almost the entirety of the ivory in trade has resulted from the unauthorized killing of elephants.

As a result of this high rate of theft, the "returns to ownership" are in fact spread across a wide variety of entities, rather than just the legal owner. It was noted in Chapter 1 that there exists a high degree of rent dispersion in the case of the ivory from the African elephant. Of the $50 million of aggregate raw ivory trade, prices received in most African markets indicate that only 10–20 per cent is appropriated by the actual harvesters in Africa, whether they are poachers selling in the black market or state governments selling off confiscated stocks.

Where does the remainder of this revenue flow to? A wide variety of individuals capture the rest: local agents and officials paid to look the other way, high government officials paid for export documentation, local traders who finance poachers and collect ivory, and international traders who move the ivory to Asia for carving.

The dispersion of the returns from the ivory over such a wide group decreases the incentive for any one of these owners (in the sense of an expected revenue flow) to attempt to invest in the resource. It is clear that this is happening in the case of many of the elephant populations, but why is it occurring? In legal parlance, the *de jure* owner of the resource is the government of the range state, while it is apparent that the beneficial interest in that same resource is divided between a wide group of individuals. This high rate of property theft is very puzzling. It is difficult to understand why the legal owner of a resource with hard currency value would allow its wholesale conversion; its high commercial value should generate incentives to protect it as well as to poach it. Why does not, or cannot, the government act in order to unite the two interests in the resource?

One possible answer is the intervention of the current rent-holders to prevent the merging of these interests. The majority of recent rents have very likely been flowing to the international traders in ivory, primarily the Hong Kong entities. If the range states were successful at appropriating ivory rents, this would effectively disenfranchise the Hong Kong traders. To combat this, the traders need only enrich a few selected members of any range state government (in an aggregate amount far less than the total rents they receive) in order to allow the current state of affairs to continue.

This phenomenon may also be conceived of as the result of inappropriate domestic property regimes. In effect, the traders are able to acquire the state's rights for a fraction of their value by purchasing them from a few of its legal owners rather than from all (i.e. all of the citizens of the state). From the official's perspective, there is no reason to decline the offer, as the property shows no return to him otherwise; he is unable to seek out a competitive price by marketing the ivory publically. Therefore, the officials who do license the sale of ivory must rely on existing connections. Some evidence for this proposition exists in the form of the inability of Japan to secure direct purchasing agreements with the African range states in the past; the Japanese trade has long complained that the Hong Kong traders have had a lock on the raw ivory trade flowing from Africa.[9]

Another possibility is that the range states do not feel that they are able to operate elephant management as a revenue-generating industry for foreign policy reasons. Unlike other natural resources, wildlife utilization invokes ethical and emotional considerations. To illustrate the potentially negative impact of such considerations on wildlife management, consider the observation that a number of range states are successful producers of a variety of other commodities, consumed primarily in the industrial countries. Most of these commodities are managed reasonably well, and certainly the flow of rents is carefully guarded. It would be considered most odd if any of these other commodities were treated as open-access resources: one does not expect to find tin mines or tea plantations open to the public. On the other hand, there are few in the international community who believe it immoral to hold tea in captivity or to sell tin in international trade.

The strength of such international sentiment is probably generated by the observed slaughter of elephants. When that slaughter is conducted by poachers, this sentiment is a constructive force for the maintenance of elephants (particularly when investments in management programmes follow as a result). But when the slaughter is conducted through a controlled culling expedition by a team from the range state's management programme, foreign intervention in such activities is very destructive. Culling is a fundamental component of any population management endeavour and it is one of the primary means by which the government ultimately obtains its revenue from the animals. If this step is unavailable to the state for foreign policy reasons, then it makes little sense to operate the remainder of the elephant management programme. Without this programme the poachers' progress is unimpeded, and the slaughter continues nonetheless.

This theory appears to fit the facts rather well. If in the foreign ministries throughout Africa the government-sponsored culling of elephant herds is seen as an unrealistic alternative, then the next most profitable solution is to harvest the resource passively. This is accomplished by the implementation of lax herd-monitoring programmes (which allow poaching to occur on a large scale) combined with more serious domestic trade-monitoring programmes (which allow confiscations to occur). This is close to the system in operation in most of the range states. Although 17 range states submitted plans to trade government ivory in 1987, only three of them made any provision for government culling operations. The remainder relied on expected confiscations for their ivory production. These states are profiting from the ivory trade without having to undertake the stigma of an elephant culling operation. Such arms-length management of elephants disperses rents and wreaks havoc on the populations.

Previous Attempts at International Regulation

For a variety of reasons, most domestic management programmes have been unsuccessful at constructively channelling the high-powered demand for elephant ivory into the conservation of stocks. It has been readily apparent for many years that other measures would be necessary in order to attempt to stem the tide of receding populations throughout most of eastern, central and western Africa. The initial attempt at an international resolution to this problem has been focused on the regulation of the trade in products from the species. It has now been in existence since 1975 and it provides an interesting case study in the predictable failure of a scheme of international regulation.

The Convention on International Trade in Endangered Species of Flora and Fauna (CITES) was signed by 21 states in 1973, and came into force in 1975 on subsequent ratification. There are now over 100 signatories, making it one of the most heavily subscribed international treaties in existence.[10]

The mechanism by which the treaty attempts to regulate international trade is the CITES permit system. Species listed in the appendices to the convention must receive pre-clearance from the exporting state's management authority prior to export; each importing state is under obligation to assure that each specimen is accompanied by such a permit. The parties must submit annual reports to the Secretariat, detailing the trade which occurred in listed species.

The conditions of importation vary, depending on the type of Appendix listing (see p. 21). The import of an Appendix I species is not allowed if it is to be used for "primarily commercial purposes". An Appendix II listing merely requires that the importing state require prior presentation of an export certificate. The African elephant was listed on Appendix II at the initial Conference of the Parties to CITES in 1976.

Almost immediately it was recognized that the machinery of CITES Appendix II was inadequate for the task of regulating the trade in elephant ivory. The 1983 Conference of the Parties to CITES (Gabarone) directed the technical committee to draw up a system for controlling the trade in ivory. The result was the adoption of the Management Quota System in 1985 under Conference Resolution 5.12.

The Management Quota System attempted to devise an international enforcement mechanism for the implementation of domestic management policies. Its basic components are as follows. Each range state was to formulate a management programme for the utilization of its elephant stock and then submit an annual quota of tusk production to the Secretariat. The exporting state was then under an obligation to notify the Secretariat of any export authorized under this quota, and it was required to mark the tusk indelibly to identify its quota number. The Secretariat was to act as an information conduit in the network. It was to receive information on quotas and permits from exporting states, and then convey the same on request to importers. Importing states were to accept only ivory shipments originating from states with non-zero quotas under the Management Quota System, after verifying the authenticity of export documents with the Secretariat.[11]

The concept motivating the system was the creation of incentives for each state to prepare an elephant-management programme. Ideally, no trade would be allowed unless a management programme was constructed which resulted in a projectable ivory offtake – the annual Management Quota. Once such a quota was derived, it was to be externally enforceable by the importing states.[12]

As an endeavour to constrict ivory flows to sustainable offtake levels, this attempt at regulation was hugely unsuccessful. There are many contributing factors but one sufficient reason for this failure: the absence of any constraint on the issuance of ivory documentation by the range states.

The underlying objective in creating any ivory documentation system, such as the Management Quota System, is the development of a method by which the state might exclusively appropriate all of the returns from ivory takings within its territory. The importing states' prohibition on all undocumented ivory vests the range state's actual document with the commercial value of the ivory to which it is affiliated; without that document, the ivory is relatively valueless (as non-importable). Thus, the documentation system in effect reduces monitoring costs because now the poachers must come to the government, rather than the government pursuing the poachers. That is, any taker of ivory must report to the government and secure a document in order to give the ivory the majority of its commercial value. Such a mechanism can make a significant contribution to the enforceability of a state's rights in its elephant populations.

To a large extent, this system merely transfers the value of the ivory to the document; thus, in order to constrain the flow of ivory, constraints on the availability of these documents become crucial to their effectiveness. To give effect to such constraints, the capacity for each state to issue this documentation must be verifiably constrained. Each state would recognize the market value of these documents once they have been received. Although it would also be apparent to each state that unrestricted documentation sales would do damage to the entire system (perhaps even resulting in the licensing of the trade in its own poached ivory!), without verifiability there is little likelihood that none of the other range states would succumb.

Non-verifiable transfers of ivory documentation are easily accomplished under the Management Quota System, merely by selling blank export permits; many examples of these operations occurring are noted in the section on "International Regulation", p. 120. This does not constitute an indictment of "African corruption"; it is the system itself which creates this market. Any state which refuses to engage in such sales is foregoing the benefit of the transaction without the assurance of receiving reciprocal benefits from other range states. Verifiable constraints on the issuance of ivory documentation were necessary conditions for the success of the system. The ultimate outcome of such a system is a complete lack of constraint on the flow of the resource.

A more obvious failing of the system was the "worked ivory loophole". Although all readily recognizable elephant products were intended to be regulated by the Management Quota System, in fact, the governments of most of the importing states did not attempt to regulate anything other than whole tusks. This is primarily attributable to the misconceived notion of constructing the regulatory system around tusk quotas. Lacking permits, a trader was only required to carve a tusk into several smaller pieces in order to evade the entire system. This loophole to the creation of several off-shore carving centres, as in the United Arab Emirates, where Chinese carvers worked ivory only to the extent necessary to enable its import into Hong Kong and Japan. Again, this patently obvious loophole destroyed the incentives for rigorous implementation by any trading state. There was little reason to invest significantly in a system so obviously defective.

The African range states readily recognized the worthlessness of investing in the Management Quota System. Of the 30 range states which indicated their willingness to comply with an international regulatory system, an average of 14 submitted annual quotas during the operation of the system. This figure actually overstates compliance with the objectives of the system, as only six states submitted quotas which were not based solely on expected confiscations of ivory.[13] The carving states also demonstrated their disdain for the system. Hong Kong, the most significant carving centre, maintained its worked ivory loophole right up until the end, positively encouraging the flow of ivory to its shores and developing huge stockpiles (currently estimated at over 500 tonnes). It is less certain to what extent the ivory-consuming states invested in the support of the system (through increased monitoring and enforcement), but it is clear (see below) that quite a lot of undetected smuggling into these centres was occurring. In sum, there was no incentive for any party to invest in this system as it was clear that there would be no expected return to those investments.

This then is indicative of the Management Quota System's failure to address satisfactorily the problem of creating incentives to obtain both agreement and implementation from the necessary parties. Not even the producing states were provided with sufficient incentives to implement the system. In a domestic regime of regulation, the failure to produce such incentives can be compensated for by the substitution of monitoring and enforcement, i.e. a police force. As this option does not exist in international law, the system foundered on this point alone.

A failed regulatory system can however be worse than none at all. Initially, it was clear that the CITES system was having no positive effect regarding the constriction of the flows of ivory in international trade; the registered levels of trade were reaching record highs. This was not the case after 1986; since then, official records (i.e. CITES documents and customs statistics) have documented dramatic reductions in the ivory trade. This cannot be the result of the Management Quota System, for the reasons given above. In addition, the estimated overall rate of population decline has not slowed in this period. In fact, these documented reductions in the ivory trade are the negative side of regulation. They result because these records cannot contain information on smuggled shipments, and the incentives to engage in smuggling operations have been increasing since international regulation came into being. This perverse side-effect of regulation, i.e. the generation of incentives for the creation of a blackmarket, is readily discernible from previous records. Throughout the era of international regulation, the ivory trade has always reacted to evade the system.

Up to 1981, only about 60 per cent of the monitored international trade was flowing through CITES states; the majority of the remainder was routed directly to Japan, then not a party to CITES. In that year, Japan acceded to the convention and the trade was then rerouted through Belgium, until its accession in 1983. After that, a number of Asian countries (Singapore, Macau and Taiwan in particular) became entrepôts for the ivory trade. Japan continued to allow shipments of ivory (from these states and others) without proper CITES documentation until new regulations were put into effect in

Table 5.1: Shifting of ivory trade routes, 1979–88 (tonnes)

	CITES	non-CITES (Asia)	non-CITES (non-Asia)	Total
1979	552 (56%)	288 (Japan)	139	979
1980	619 (64%)	270 (Japan)	77	966
1981	763 (85%)	22	110	895
1982	639 (72%)	35	216 (Belgium)	890
1983	718 (71%)	44	255 (Belgium)	1,017
1984	556 (78%)	192 (Singapore)	0	710
1985	295 (42%)	162 (Singapore)	254	711
1986	206 (35%)	399 (Singapore)	0	587
1987	317 (78%)	80 (Taiwan)	0	370
1988	299 (98%)	4	0	303

Source: Adapted from R. Luxmoore, J. Caldwell and L. Hithersay, "Comparisons of CITES and Customs Statistics on the International Trade in Raw Ivory", Report to the Ivory Trade Review Group (1989).

1985. In 1986 Singapore acceded to CITES and was allowed to register its stockpile of some 300 tonnes of ivory, which were then allowed as "legal" ivory. Thus, in this way, the ivory trade had shifted away from CITES states and towards non-CITES states throughout the early 1980s, while maintaining consistently high levels of trade.

This pattern of evasion was readily detectable throughout this period from the customs records of non-party states; such detection is now less feasible since most of the consumer states have become parties to CITES. The lower levels of documented trade since 1986 are probably attributable as much to lower rates of detection as to lower levels of trade. Rather than shifting the trade to non-CITES havens, the ivory shippers have the additional option of refusing to register shipments as ivory, i.e. smuggling. Most shipments move by container, with little possibility of inspection by customs agents; no incentives exist for manufacturing states to monitor imports carefully in order to enforce this legislation against the interests of their carving industries. It is almost certainly the case that a significant portion of the trade went underground during the latter part of the decade. The fact that CITES and customs records converged during this period is probably more of an indication of the amount of trade that has disappeared from sight than a sign that the illegal trade has been halted.[14]

Recent attempts at international regulation of the flows of ivory have failed miserably. If flows have been reduced in this decade, the primary reason is the sharp reductions in the stocks which are available to be drawn upon. The Management Quota System was a well-intended idea, yet it was dead from the start.

Is it possible to construct a plan for international regulation which itself generates incentives to agreement and implementation, at each level of the trade? The next section addresses these issues.

International Regulation and the African Elephant

International regulation is always a problematic affair. The primary distinction between national regimes and international ones is the absence of a monitoring and enforcement structure. International contracts do not in general depend for enforcement upon a police force which has the responsibility of monitoring the performance of obligations, nor do they have penalties enforceable against recalcitrant states which might be discovered to be in violation.

For this reason it is very difficult to enter into international contracts with regard to internal matters, since it is not possible to verify the state's performance of its obligations. An international contract operates in the same way as does any mutually benefical exchange: each party must be able to observe the benefit which it receives from other parties' performances as a precondition to its willingness to undertake its own. If the performances of other parties are not visible, then there is little reason to expect such contracts to generate much change in the states' courses of action.

Failures of international regimes of regulation are predictable when solutions are not found for this fundamental problem of international regulation, that is, the creation of incentives for unanimous acceptance and implementation of the regime. There are two sub-parts to this problem. First, it is necessary to construct a regime which minimizes the number of necessary contracting parties; greater numbers imply greater transactions costs and less chance of unanimous acceptance. Second, some means of monitoring the performance of contractual obligations is absolutely necessary for implementation to occur. The absence of these criteria, and the consequent failure of the system, are now explored in regard to the CITES Management Quota System, and an idealised system consistent with these criteria is described.

Failure of the Management Quota Sysem
The failure of the Management Quota System was a failure of

acceptance and implementation by the necessary states. If it had been implemented in any form approximating to that which was intended, it would have been effective in greatly reducing poaching pressures on elephant stocks. Why then did it fail so utterly?

First, there was a predictable failure arising from this system's dependence for its effectiveness on the regulation of the intermediate (manufacturing) tier of the ivory industry. This is because there was no fixity to this stage of the enterprise, and so it was difficult to restrict the number of necessary contracting parties. In addition, there was no incentive to constrict trade in ivory at this level; it was against the manufacturing states' interests to invest in the enforcement of this regime – it simply reduced the amount of manufacturing activity available.

Thus, the Management Quota System required nearly universal acceptance of the scheme as a prerequisite for its success. And it required this of a vast majority of states (whose actual or potential involvement in the industry was restricted to manufacturing) for whom the regulation was necessarily against self-interest. This is of course impossible to achieve, and thus failure was predictable in this regard alone.

A second source of predictable failure was the absence of a credible monitoring structure. In order for one party to the contract to engage in self-sacrifice, this sacrifice must be demonstrable to the other parties and reciprocating benefits must then be demonstrably conferred by other parties.

The Management Quota System simply failed to provide any element of verifiability. Empowering each of the range states to issue any number of these documents that they desired rendered them useless as verification papers. The CITES documents, left blank, would be convertible to hard currencies in the export-permit market. Alternatively, all that was necessary was the submission of a substantial quota for the next year and then the sale of the documents for these amounts; one state even amended its quota in mid-year when it was informed that it had put more documents into circulation than its previous quota allowed.[15]

Again, this is *not* meant as an indictment of officialdom in Africa. These activities were entirely predictable from the structure of the Management Quota System. Given the creation of a document necessary for the importation of ivory into the hard-currency consumer states, it is clear that a market for such documentation would develop. To empower each range state with the unrestricted capacity to print such documents creates a situation where it is unlikely that a shortfall of the documentation would ensue. If such a system were to succeed, the quantities of such documentation would have to be externally restricted.

In sum, the Management Quota System failed because it depended on states taking actions against self-interest. It was dependent upon the goodwill of manufacturing states for enforcement activities with regard to legislation, which was clearly contrary to their economic interest; this was not likely to occur. In addition, if one such state was bludgeoned into acquiescence, three or four more would be created. With regard to range states, the absence of credible monitoring equipment made self-sacrifice nonsensical; the clear absence of systemic constraints made self-restraint an obviously charitable rather than an economical activity.

Elements of international regulation

What then are the elements of a workable system of international regulation regarding the African elephant? An attempt to assist in its conservation must solve the following two-pronged regulation problem in regard to the international regulation of domestic resources:

i) the correction of investment deficiencies – involving the determination of the probable reasons for the failure of producers to invest in the maintenance of elephant stocks, and the range of potential responses to these defects; and

ii) the construction of an enforceable system – involving the consideration of the predictable attempts of individuals (and states) to circumvent any scheme of regulation where it is in their self-interest to do so.

In addition, the solution to this problem must be considered within its relevant context: the regulation of the ivory industry by means of an *international contract*. In many instances it would not be possible to solve such a conservation problem in the context of international agreements. Such agreements depend for their execution upon self-generated incentives towards compliance. Where non-compliance is not in a state's self-interest, the agreement will fail to attain its objective. This is precisely the set of difficulties which has afflicted the previous attempts at international regulation in this area.

It should be possible to solve this problem in the case of the African elephant, however, if the defect currently preventing investment in elephant stocks is rooted in rent dispersion. In that case, the solution is the creation of an enforceable system of rent aggregation, i.e. the channelling of all rents from the sale of ivory to a single owner/controller of the elephant stock. Such a unification of the interests in the elephant population would create incentives to consider the full flow of future potential revenues from the stock, and thus to invest in its maintenance.

How can such an enforceable system be instituted? It may be possible in the case of the African elephant because there exists an economic incentive for enforceable joint action by the range states. This is the direct result of the demand inelasticity which ivory sales have exhibited. Under these circumstances, the profit maximizing action to take is the formation of a joint marketing agreement for the purpose of constricting the flow of ivory. In short, the demand elasticity for ivory exhibited in Japan is in the same neighbourhood as that of petroleum (0.5 to 0.7); the incentives to engage in joint marketing should be approximately the same as those affecting the oil-producing states.

There are two reasons why such an agreement will usually fail. The first was alluded to previously: there are incentives for producers to cheat on any such agreement. The second reason is that the consumers of such goods generally want the agreement to fail, as it constrains consumption and raises prices.

In short, an international agreement to constrain production can only be successful in the following circumstances:

i) if the demand elasticity indicates joint gains to producers' constrained production;
ii) if a focal-point solution exists to indicate the basis upon which such quotas should be distributed (i.e. an obvious basis for the distribution of the gains from cooperation exists); and
iii) if consumer states are willing to monitor and enforce the agreement for the producers.

These conditions all exist in the context of the ivory trade. As emphasized previously, ivory demand is significantly non-responsive to price in Japan, the primary consumer. The focal-point solution available for the determination of annual ivory quotas is the sustainable offtake of ivory from existing elephant stocks. Such a solution is desirable because it provides the *consumer* states with incentives to support the *producers*' agreement. That is, in order to maintain a legal and stable trade, the consumer states are willing to undertake the expense of the enforcement mechanism for a producers' agreement based upon sustainable offtake. The consumer states' involvement then supplies the external verification mechanism necessary for the enforcement of the producer states' agreement. Thus, all of the conditions for a successful international agreement are present. Both producers and consumers win in the long run; a sustainable equilibrium is obtained and the industry is stabilized.

Again, this is not the case with regard to an agreement which is dependent upon manufacturers for implementation, for their objectives are countervailing. The manufacturers are interested in ivory sales on account of the value which is added by virtue of mixing labour with ivory. As ivory flows are constricted, the demands for their services are reduced and their profits are consequently reduced. What is more, any revenues resulting from scarcity in the quantity of ivory products on the market accrue to the manufacturer, not the ivory carver. Thus there are no incentives for the manufacturer to enforce the agreement, and plenty of disincentives toward non-compliance.

A number of different types of systems might be utilized to implement this solution. An "ivory currency" system would have the range states agree ivory quotas in kilograms and then distribute non-counterfeitable currency units in those amounts. The consumer states would then disallow imports in the absence of a currency unit for each kilo of ivory imported, worked or unworked. Alternatively, the producer states might launch an exclusive "ivory exchange". Such an exchange would only take ivory in sustainable amounts from range state governments. Consumer states would then enter into exclusive purchasing agreements with the exchange.

The reason why any of these mechanisms might be effective in the case of the elephant is that they address both elements of the regulation problem set forth above. First, each of these approaches aggregates revenues by the elimination of the middlemen, and actually acts to increase the price per kilogram of ivory. Thus, the incentives to invest in elephant stocks are restored and enhanced. Incentives to invest sustainably are reinforced by gearing quotas to the available sustainable offtake. Thus, the investment defects element of the regulation problem is soluble.

The enforceability element is solved by two innovations. First, the system has incentives to agreement. It is structured so that all necessary parties gain from agreement. The range states receive higher rents for their resources, and the consumer states sign on in order to foster the sustainability of the resource. No other states are required to undertake any enforcement necessary to the system. In particular, these incentives take into consideration the differences between the various range states' management programmes and reward them accordingly; there is no incentive to abstain from agreement as is currently the case. Second, once agreement is obtained, enforcement is strictly an external affair; there is no reliance upon self-monitoring. Both quotas and documentation are created within the system, and monitoring is conducted by the consumer states. There is no unrestrained discretion left with any state which would cause the agreement to degenerate, as has been the case in the past.

Therefore, the regulation problem is soluble in the case of the African elephant by means of a number of different mechanisms. This will not always be the case with regard to the international regulation of domestic resources, but it happens that the characteristics of the elephant make it possible for such an agreement to be effective.

Alternative Mechanisms for International Regulation

There are a number of different approaches available for the implementation of the solution described above. Three of them are the ivory exchange system, the ivory currency system and the ivory tax system. All of them are logically identical in many respects, that is, they operate by increasing the returns from ivory to well-managed populations. The legal problems raised by this manner of regulation are primarily the following:

i) the certification problem, i.e. how to distinguish between a well-managed state population and one that is not so; and

ii) the counterfeit problem, i.e. how to distinguish between a correctly certified piece of ivory and one that is not so.

The three possible systems will now be described in greater detail, with particular regard to their differences in the resolution of these two legal problems.

The Ivory Exchange system
One means for controlling a sustainable-yield ivory trade would be through the establishment of an Ivory Exchange. The essential principles of the Exchange would be to encourage exclusive agreements by consumer countries to purchase all ivory through the Exchange, and to restrict the number of suppliers to those producers who conform with some sustainability criterion.

The critical consuming countries that must execute "exclusive purchasing agreements" would be the three historically significant end-users: the USA, the EEC and Japan. It would also be necessary to secure the cooperation of the primary manufacturing centres: Hong Kong and China. These parties would be required to comply with the Exchange Rules applicable to consumers, which would specify importation and monitoring procedures. With the verifiable cooperation of these parties, it would be possible to create substantial incentives to secure membership in the Exchange.

Range states would have to apply for membership in the Exchange based on a demonstrated record of sustainable management capability. This would require the demonstration of several years of documented maintenance of existing elephant populations. Once membership was approved, the producer state must additionally agree to the Exchange Rules. These Rules must set strict ceilings on the sale of confiscated ivory, determine ivory production limits (based on sustainable yields) and price floors and, most importantly, provide for independent audits of members' continuing compliance with the membership criteria.

The Exchange itself would hold the auctions of the ivory tendered by member states, and arrange for its certification and transportation to the consumer states. As mentioned above, the Exchange would be responsible for the creation of Exchange Rules for both producers and consumers, and it would also be charged with the responsibility of conducting annual audits of members' compliance with them.[16]

The ivory currency system

The ivory currency system would use the biennial CITES conference of the parties as its administrative centre. It would provide for the establishment of individual quotas of ivory by a technical committee, in accordance with principles of sustainable stocks. The sales of these quotas would be licensed by means of ivory currency notes, which would be non-counterfeitable currency documents issued immediately after the conference to the range states. The consumer states would be charged with preventing imported ivory flows in the absence of an accompanying currency note.

This system would hinge on the commitment of the consumer states to its enforcement; an important component would be an express commitment of resources to ivory import monitoring by the primary consumer states. Once such a commitment inhered in a number of states representing the majority of ivory purchasing power (e.g. the USA, the EEC and Japan), the incentives for producer states to participate would be very great. Once again, consumer state incentives to participate would have to arise from the demonstrated effectiveness of the system.

Range states would be allowed ivory currency notes in amounts consistent with the kilograms of ivory which might be harvested sustainably from their elephant stocks. These notes may then be used to license elephant harvests in their states. The incentive to manage sustainably arises from the price differential between licensed ivory and ivory for which no certificates exist; if the consumer states invest substantial amounts in monitoring imports, the value of non-certificated ivory should be a small fraction of licensed ivory.

Consumer states would monitor ivory imports in kilograms, not pieces, and thus the same ivory currency note is acceptable whether the ivory is worked or raw.

The Conference of the Parties would be required to appoint an ongoing technical committee, responsible for the monitoring of range states' populations and the determination of biennial quotas (for submission for the approval of the Conference). There would also have to be secretariat personnel involved in the monitoring process in the consumer state customs operation; this would be necessary for the detection of counterfeit currency and the coordination of all monitoring operations.

The ivory tax system
The ivory tax system would involve the agreement of all primary consumers of ivory to the imposition of a substantial tax on the importation of ivory. The tax receipts would then be accumulated in an African Elephant Conservation Fund, and subsequently returned to the range states.

The primary consumer states would have to agree to implement a uniform tax on ivory imports in a single trade agreement. This tax must be computed with the objective of reducing aggregate demand to sustainable levels. In addition, the signatories would also have to pledge a uniform (per tonne imported) allocation of funds to customs operations for the express purpose of the detection of ivory smuggling. The incentive to enter into such an agreement would come from the perceived effectiveness of such a system in the maintenance of elephant stocks.

The receipts must then be accumulated in a fund for the conservation of the African elephant. These should then be redistributed to African states in inverse proportion to the rate of mining of stocks which is occurring in those states; that is, if elephant stocks are stable, then large compensation should be paid from the fund. Of course, such payments must also take into consideration the relative sizes of elephant populations in the range states, and thus increase proportionately with the increase in sustainable flows of ivory. The incentives for range states in such a scheme are to meet the attainment criteria of the African Elephant Conservation Board in order to receive compensation from the fund.

The African Elephant Conservation Board would be an international commission established by the trade agreement. Its role would be threefold. First, it would analyse the demand and trade in ivory in order to establish ivory taxes and customs dedications, in sums sufficient to generate the African Elephant Conservation Fund. Second, it must establish clear management attainment criteria, with attendant compensation bonuses, for the encouragement of sustainable management. Third, it must coordinate these two activities in a way that balances its accounts.

Conclusion

Each of these trading mechanisms fits the criteria for the solution of the problem of regulation outlined above. In fact, logically they are identical; they are three different methods of increasing the returns to sustainable management through the device of external monitoring. That is, each mechanism operates by encouraging investment by range states in the preservation of elephant populations, by means of increasing the return to ivory derived from well-managed populations. Enforceability is provided for by the establishment of external monitoring capabilities with regard to each party's performance. Effectiveness is assured by ensuring that each party is required to take action only where it is in its self-interest to do so. Only through the use of one of these mechanisms can the international regulation of this resource be effective.

Notes

1. See A. Burrill and I. Douglas-Hamilton, African Elephant Database Project – Final Report, 1987, GRID Case Study Series No. 2; I. Douglas-Hamilton, African Elephant Population Study Report, 1988; I. Douglas-Hamilton and R. Barnes, "Elephant Numbers and Trends", Summary Report to the Ivory Trade Review Group, (1989).
2. Renewable Resources Assessment Group, "The Impact of the Ivory Trade on the African Elephant Population", Report to the Ivory Trade Review Group (1989).
3. Not only do most African states already have laws asserting "exclusive rights" in the elephant populations, but many of them have long had "bans" (of hunting or the trade or both) in their national laws for years. IUCN Environmental Law Centre, *African Wildlife Laws*, (IUCN: Gland, 1985).
4. The report by the Renewable Resources Assessment Group in the Final Report of the Ivory Trade Review Group summarizes the literature on the population characteristics of the African Elephant. See RRAG, op. cit. (Note 2).

5. The annual offtake in Kruger has been around 2,500 kg from a standing stock of approximately 24,000 kg of ivory in the managed herd. See R.B. Martin, *Establishment of African Ivory Export Quotas and Associated Control Procedures*, Report to the CITES Secretariat, (1985).

6. D. Cumming, R. Martin and S. Taylor, in *The Status and Conservation of Africa's Elephants and Rhinos*, (eds. D. Cumming and P. Jackson), (IUCN: Gland, 1984). They found the total conservation budgets available in 15 African states to be $44,770,000, ranging from $24,000 in Niger to $13,000,000 in Zimbabwe. This represents an expenditure per staff member of $4,330, or $52 per km^2 of conservation areas.

7. A study of the relationship between government spending on conservation and the change in rhinoceros numbers showed a close correlation. Relative spending rates explained 68 per cent of the variance in rhinoceros population declines. The predicted requisite spending for 0 per cent change was $230 per km^2. Another regression computed with regard to elephant population declines demonstrated a similar relationship, but with a less reliable fit (32 per cent of variance explained). N. Leader-Williams and S. Albon, "Allocation of Resources for Conservation", *Nature*, vol. 336, (December 1988), p. 533. This evidence conforms quite closely with the "folklore" that $200 per km^2 is the necessary spending level for adequate conservation. R.H.V. Bell and J. Clarke, "Funding and Financial Control", in R. Bell and E. McShane-Caluzi (eds.) *Conservation and Wildlife Management in Africa*, (Office of the Peace Corps, 1984). This figure will, of course, vary quite considerably from state to state, depending on demand pressures and exchange rates amongst other things, but the magnitude of amounts required will remain substantial nonetheless.

8. Rowan Martin gives an excellent description of the idealized workings of a CAMPFIRE programme in this paper. The primary focus is the involvement of local communities in the development of tourism, wildlife and forestry resources. Giving these communities a say in the operation of these programmes creates new interest in the development of these areas. See R.B. Martin, "Communal Area Management Plan for Indigenous Resources (Project Campfire)", in Bell and McShane-Caluzi, op. cit.(Note 7).

9. One of the leading ivory traders in Hong Kong, Mr Wang of the Compagnie Franco-Chinoise, claims that this is due to "special connections with African dealers". See "The Ivory Crisis", *Asiaweek*, (5 August 1988).

10. For a description of the history and operation of The Convention on International Trade in Endangered Species, see S. Lyster, *International Wildlife Law*, (Grotius: London, 1985); or W. Wijnstekers, *The Evolution of CITES*, (CITES Secretariat: Lausanne, 1988).

11. The general guidelines for the implementation of the CITES Management Quota System were reported in a CITES Secretariat publication, *Ivory Trade Control Procedures*, (Nov. 1985).

12. The motivating principles underlying the system are set forth in R.

Martin, J. Caldwell and J. Barzdo, *African Elephants, CITES and the Ivory Trade*, Report to the CITES Secretariat (1986).

13. The extent of compliance with the Management Quota System was derided in the 1987 report by the African Elephant and Rhinoceros Specialists Group, *Elephant Population Estimates, Trends, Ivory Quotas and Harvests*. Examples include: "In one country, where there is no policy to cull, crop or control elephants, large numbers in each of these categories have been entered . . . This year the quota is for 18,000 tusks, of which about 7,000 will arise from elephants dying in the quota year, 2,000 are current stocks and 9,000 will be confiscated during the year. This implies that poaching cannot be prevented."

14. I.S.C. Parker, *The Raw Ivory Trade, 1979–87*, Report to the CITES Secretariat, (1987). This report argues that this has been the primary effect of international regulation.

15. Parker cites Tanzania, Sudan and Uganda as states which provided permits "in blank" in order to license trade in the Burundi stockpile. He also provides numerous examples of shipments occurring under "speculative permits", purchased from range states to be matched up with illegal ivory shipments. He estimates that about 250 tonnes of ivory (over one-third of the entire ivory in trade) was processed in this way during the first two years of the Management Quota System. Parker, op. cit. p. 122 (Note 14).

16. The Ivory Exchange System was presented as an option by the International Union for the Conservation of Nature at the Lausanne Conference of the Parties to CITES. It is simply not possible to secure the attention of all the relevant parties in the two-week timespan of such a meeting. For this reason, it is important that work commence immediately on the construction of such an option. (T. Swanson and D. Pearce "International Regulation of the Ivory Trade: The Ivory Exchange", Report to the International Union for the Conservation of Nature, 1989.)

6 LOOKING TO THE FUTURE: POLICY OPTIONS TO SAVE THE ELEPHANT

Current CITES Regulation: The Appendix I Listing

The Seventh Meeting of the Conference of the Parties to CITES occurred in Lausanne, Switzerland in October 1989. At that time the parties voted by 76–15 in favour of the so-called "Somalia Amendment" to list the African elephant on Appendix I. This proposal moved all populations of the species to Appendix I, with the proviso that any range state could apply to a panel of experts for the selective downlisting (to Appendix II) of its elephant population. (See p. 21.)

Even before the Lausanne Conference of the Parties, moves had been afoot to ban the trade in ivory. The USA had adopted the African Elephant Conservation Act of 1988, which proscribed *inter alia* imports of ivory from any state which was not a member of CITES, or which traded in non-CITES ivory. In addition, that Act also allowed for the establishment of an African Elephant Conservation Fund from which direct subsidies to well-managed programmes might be allowed. Then, on 9 June 1989 and after considerable public pressure, the USA banned all imports of ivory pending the resolution of the Conference of the Parties in Lausanne. Several other states and the EEC shortly followed suit.[1]

The only other major ivory consumer, Japan, imposed a ban on the import of ivory from non-producer states on 19 June 1989. That is, Japan agreed to trade in ivory only with African states directly, and not with intermediate parties. From 13 September Japan imposed a temporary import ban on all ivory, effective until after the CITES Conference.

The Appendix I listing under the terms of the Somali proposal has been supported by all of the historically important consumers of ivory. The USA, the EEC and Japan all continued with their bans in place after the Lausanne meeting. The USA has additionally listed the African elephant, with the exceptions of the populations in Zimbabwe, Botswana and South Africa, as an endangered species under the terms of the US Endangered Species Act, with effect from 16 February 1990; this effectively prohibits all internal trade in ivory from endangered populations. The Appendix I listing has the same effect within the EEC.

The Somalia Amendment evolved through four days of discussions of alternative proposals. The pursuit of unanimity of acceptance was centred around three separate proposed amendments to the Appendix I listing. One proposal supported a split Appendix I/II listing, which would allow only Botswana, Zimbabwe and South Africa in Appendix II because they have healthy elephant populations and effective management programmes – provided that these countries also would hold to a zero ivory quota until the next CITES Conference. However, a counter-proposal from the southern African countries insisted that eight countries – Botswana, Zimbabwe, South Africa, Mozambique, Malawi and Zambia, as well as two CITES non-Parties, Angola and Namibia – stay in Appendix II. An additional central African proposal requested that Gabon, Cameroon and Congo also remain in Appendix II. Neither counter-proposal accepted a trade moratorium until the next CITES Conference.

In a series of votes on these proposals, each of the above proposals was rejected together with the "pure" Appendix I uplisting. Then the Somalia Amendment, allowing selective downlisting, was voted on and accepted by the Conference of the Parties.

The Appendix I listing proscribes all imports of elephant products for primarily commercial purposes, with the possible exception of sport hunting trophies. Besides ivory, this regulation also captures elephant hides within its ambit, which constitute a fair portion of the revenues generated within the elephant management programmes. Elephant trophy hunting is a disproportionately important source of income and one of the mainstays of local wildlife utilization schemes in countries such as Zimbabwe. However, under USA and EEC law, the future of elephant trophy importation is also in doubt.[2]

It was roundly agreed that the previous system of international regulation, i.e. the Management Quota System, was a total failure. CITES has now moved into a new era of international regulation by means of the institution of a formalized international ban on the trade in elephant products. The prospects for the success of this measure are no better; in terms of international regulation for sustainable elephant populations, the situation has gone from bad to worse.

The Impact of an Ivory Trade Ban

An ivory trade ban, as an attempt to increase elephant stocks, must satisfy the regulation problem set out in Chapter 5. That is, as with any attempt to solve this problem by means of international regulation, it must adequately address two issues: the problem of insufficient investment and the problem of insufficient enforcement (i.e. inadequate acceptance and implementation).

An ivory trade ban does not address this regulation problem very well. In regard to the enforcement element of the problem, it is apparent that there are few incentives for unanimous agreement to such a proposal, and thus the taking of reservations (i.e. countries removing themselves from a regulatory scheme) was a predictable response to the policy. An absolute ban is very sensible from the viewpoint of a state such as Kenya, whose elephant stocks are valued much more highly for their tourism-generating capacity than for their ivory. This is not so for other states, such as Zimbabwe, which have invested large sums in the management of their wildlife and must show a return to justify future investments. Predictably, Kenya was a primary proponent of the Appendix I listing, while Zimbabwe has refused to agree to this amendment and thus has unilaterally taken a reservation. Other producer states have also listed reservations, including South Africa (whose elephant populations are stable), Malawi, Zambia and Botswana (whose elephant stocks have also been rising, against the continental downwards trend).[3]

It is also to be anticipated that the states which have relatively large vested interests in the manufacture of ivory, as opposed to its final consumption, would resist an ivory trade ban. The historically important ivory-carving states are all Asian, of which India, China, Hong Kong and Japan are the most prominent. These countries have typically represented almost the entirety of the global ivory-carving industry. Two of them, China and Hong Kong, have entered reservations.[4] One, India, had declared its intention to enter a reservation, but failed to do so by the time of the deadline (18 January 1990) by reason of a bureaucratic error.[5] Only Japan amongst the major carving states acceded to the ivory trade ban, and of course Japan is the only one of the group which fulfils a dual role as carver and consumer.

Therefore, it appears that the vast majority of states have made decisions which are consistent with their economic self-interest, and that the trade will continue despite the ban. Southern African states have declared their intention to continue trade in ivory; Asian carvers have declared their intention to continue to carve it. The only missing piece to the puzzle is the existence of a group of final consumers with the purchasing power to drive the market; the previous consumers (the USA, the EEC and Japan) have all opted out, at least for the time being. The only other part of the world where equivalent purchasing power exists in non-CITES states is the Middle East, due to petrodollars, and the current reports are that the Southern African states are attempting to develop this market.

More likely, the greatest part of future consumption of worked ivory will occur in those countries where the demand for ivory is deeply instilled but latent due to the high price of ivory, and irrespective of the state's CITES status. The history of growth in Japanese ivory consumption parallels its income growth over the past four decades (demonstrated by an income-elasticity of 1.50). This same pattern of increasing consumption is being replicated in the newly industrializing countries of Asia: South Korea, Taiwan, Thailand and Singapore. For example, South Korea's consumption of Hong Kong worked ivory has increased by 1,000 per cent over the past decade. These states are the obvious targets for market development, especially as ivory prices fall and Asian incomes rise. There is tremendous scope for the development of new markets for worked ivory in these Asian states.

Another source of outlets for worked ivory are those states which have adopted the ban, but whose citizens still exhibit demand for the commodity; in this situation, there are substantial incentives to smuggle the ivory into those states. The difference in consumer outlook is crucial in this respect. If the consumers adopt the ban, then there is little incentive to smuggle; however, if consumers resist the ban then substantial government resources must be dedicated to its implementation. Recent evidence on the relative impact of the ban in the USA and Japan is illustrative. Prices in the USA have been falling precipitously, with some stores offering 70 per cent discounts; on the other hand, prices in Japan are rising significantly, some items have actually doubled in price.[6]

If consumers do not personally adopt the ban, as is the case in Japan, then there is a substantial incentive to smuggle the ivory into the country. Previous experience with attempted embargoes of substances which the citizenry demands indicates that success is unlikely.[7] In essence, in this situation the effectiveness of the ban is wholly dependent upon the investment of correspondingly large sums of money in the monitoring and enforcement of the import ban. Of course, there is little incentive in most consumer states to invest so heavily for the purpose of completely depriving their citizenry of the substance; the contradiction between the people's desires and the state's undertaking is made obvious.

In nations such as Japan, where substantial state resources exist for such monitoring, the consequence of this conflict in objectives is primarily likely to be small-scale smuggling. Purchases by tourists abroad and small shipments of slightly worked ivory are to be anticipated.[8] In other Asian states without the resources of Japan, the degree of evasion will be much more severe. States such as Thailand and Singapore are unlikely to commit significantly more resources for the purpose of restricting the ivory trade, because of the scarcity of resources and also because such restrictions fly in the face of their citizens' demonstrated desires. In these CITES states, it is possible to develop new markets.

In short, the enforcement difficulties with regard to a ban have been almost entirely ignored. Although the primary consumer states have agreed the change, there is no mechanism in place to police this infinitely more complicated system. A mere statement of prohibition does little to actually alter the trade, barring significant new investments to enforce the ban. There are few incentives to do so in the states which would like to continue to trade. In addition, there will be new markets developed for the ivory turned away from Japan, the USA and the EEC, and there is no capacity for monitoring this activity. Those producer states which have accepted a ban will find that significant pressures on their elephant populations will continue to persist, while they themselves are no longer allowed to trade in the ivory from their elephant herds. All of these inherent contradictions within the ban concept discourage investment in this regime. It is to be anticipated that *all* manufacturers, *many* consumers and *most* producers will not invest sufficiently in the enforcement of this system.

An unenforced ban will be tragic for the elephant. The problem is that, as the trade has always consisted of both a legal and an illegal component, banning the trade (without the simultaneous implementation of an adequate enforcement structure) will provide the incentives for expanding its illegal component. A ban will only have an impact on this component if the costs of relocating the illegal trade are very high. As discussed in previous chapters, historically the ivory trade has proven to be very fluid. The only way to increase the costs to an illegal trade would be to ensure maximum compliance with the ban, i.e. with virtually no existing or potential consumers and producers taking a reservation. The presence of reservations, combined with the absence of significant new investments in monitoring the ban, will result in the transfer of much of the formerly "legal" trade into the "illegal" sector.

Figure 6.1 illustrates this situation. The effect of the ban will be to cause initial demand, D_0, to decrease; this is the result of the exit from the market of the primary consumers: the USA, the EEC and Japan. There will be a fall in price – as is currently occurring – until demand adjusts by the entrance of new consumers (Saudi Arabia, South

Figure 6.1: The effects of an ivory ban

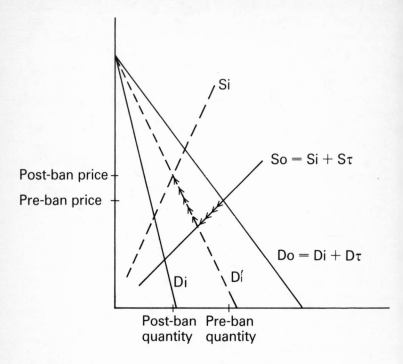

So = Supply curve before ban, illegal and legal supply (Si + Sτ)

Si = Supply curve after ban, illegal supply only

Do = Demand curve before ban, illegal and legal demand (Di + Dτ)

Di = Demand curve before ban, illegal demand only

Di′ = Demand curve after ban, illegal demand only

Source: London Environmental Economics Centre.

Korea, Taiwan). These new consumers were earlier foreclosed from the market due to the high hard currency prices then prevailing; the exit of the hard currency consumers causes prices to fall, but demand to remain strong. Previously demand had been made up of CITES-certified quantities (legal demand – D_1) and non-certified quantities (illegal demand – D_1); after the ban, virtually all ivory will be the latter. Thus, overall demand falls, but the illegal component will have actually expanded with the entrance of new consumers.

The supply side of the picture is less clearcut. As mentioned previously, there are no incentives within a ban for increased expenditures on elephant maintenance and monitoring; therefore, from this perspective, it is probable that no shift in the supply curve would occur. This is consistent with the impact of past legislative bans; most African states have previously imposed domestic bans on hunting with little observable impact on the actual ivory supplies. However, there may be a difference with this ban, in that the USA has pledged $5 million to elephant conservation measures under the African Elephant Conservation Act. It has also forgiven $300 million in debt to the non-reservation states, which would hypothetically release some $30 million of interest repayment funds for this purpose. The EEC and Japan have also contributed to elephant management efforts. If some of these funds are actually invested in elephant management practices, then the costs of poaching may increase and the supply of ivory may be restricted.

What are the combined effects of the ivory trade ban? In the short term, aggregate quantities of ivory in trade must fall to a significant extent, perhaps as much or more than 50 per cent. This is due to the exit of a substantial quantity of hard currency demand; time will be required to replace this level of consumption. In the longer term, a substantial quantity of new demand will be brought on line from states previously priced out of the market (e.g. South Korea, Taiwan, Saudi Arabia); this demand cannot completely replace the previous levels, but it will be entirely unmonitored as these states are all outside of the CITES system. In addition, some quantities of ivory will continue to find their way into Japan and other CITES states (Thailand, Singapore), by way of tourists and inadequate enforcement measures in general; these quantities will also be unmonitored. Thus, after the initial price fall and the transition to new markets, the ivory pipeline will re-open and the price of ivory will begin to rise once again (see Figure 6.1).

Therefore, under the conditions of an inadequately enforced ivory trade ban, the quantities of ivory in trade will once again be substantial, and now they will be wholly outside of regulatory control.

This is the perverse effect of regulation at work once again; regulation with ineffective enforcement measures simply encourages evasion.

However, even an effective ban is ultimately of no avail. The prohibition of trading does nothing to address the problem of insufficient investment in elephants. At the most fundamental level this is precisely the problem which must be solved. Elephant populations in Africa are competing for an allocation of resources (land, etc.) in states where substantial quantities are not easily available. In addition, burgeoning human populations in many of these states – Kenya's is currently the fastest growing population in the world – intensify the pressure on these limited resource bases. At the same time, many of these states are also becoming fully integrated within the world economy for the first time, generating rapid change and increased trade opportunities. It is within this increasingly complicated and pressurized context that the preservation of elephant populations must occur. It is not simply a matter of retaining the status quo.

Investments of resources in the retention of elephants by African states hinges upon the demonstration that sustainable management practices will with certainty yield returns over a significant term of years in the future. The decision to invest in another generation of elephants implies a commitment to maintain them over some significant portion of their 70-year lifespan. This requires a reasonably assured expectation that there will be a corresponding flow of resources deriving from their maintenance, and upon which they might depend. Tourism is one possibility, but in order to maximize the number of elephants it is necessary to capture all of the potentially appropriable value of the species. In this way, the incentives to invest in elephants are maximised.

The ivory trade ban is completely misdirected in this regard. The removal of the hard currency consumers (the USA, the EEC and Japan) from the market will certainly reduce the value of ivory, even if the quantities are *not* similarly reduced (on account of increased trade with less wealthy states – South Korea, Taiwan, Singapore). Pressures on elephant populations will continue. The costs of monitoring will remain substantial. But the overall returns to elephant management will be significantly reduced. In sum, an ivory trade ban is, in the long run, a very perverse way in which to attempt to conserve the elephant.

A Proposal for the International Regulation of the Trade

There is one positive side to the ivory trade ban. If construed as a moratorium, i.e. a temporary ban, it might provide the respite necessary for the construction and implementation of a truly effective package of regulation.

This is because the initial impact of the ban is relatively positive. That is, the wholesale removal of the USA and the EEC from the ivory market will initially cause prices to plummet and unsold stocks to clog up the trade pipeline. This creates incentives to discover new consumption outlets and trade routes, but time will be required to implement these objectives. The trade ban should provide a brief respite in the ivory wars until the system begins to flow once again and stocks are cleared out. This one-time benefit is then counterbalanced by the loss of capacity to monitor or control future flows in the ivory trade, and the loss of incentives to invest in elephant management.

The positive impact of the trade ban should be felt only once, and only at the outset of the ban; thereafter, this gain will be chipped away at by the illegal traders. If this "window" is used to positive effect, then the ban might ultimately be turned to constructive purposes. If the ban is allowed to continue unaltered, then the costs will soon overtake and subsume the one-time benefit.

What is to be done with this window of ban effectiveness? A concerted effort must be undertaken to devise and agree an enforceable package of international regulation prior to the next meeting of the Conference of the Parties which occurs in 1991.

The principles for the construction of an effective regime of international regulation have been set forth in detail in Chapter 5 above. Suffice it to say that the regulation scheme must satisfy the two elements of the regulation problem:

i) incentives to investment in elephant stocks; and
ii) incentives to enforcement, encompassing:
    a) incentives to agreement; and
    b) an external monitoring institution.

There are numerous methods by which such a system might be implemented, but they all should contain some common elements. First, the incentives to agree to reduced flows of ivory between the range states (and thus reduced harvests of elephants) are derived from the demonstrated inelasticity of demand for ivory. That is, there is an incentive to develop an enforceable ivory-producers' cartel; reduced flows would generate greater rents to the producers.

Second, the basis for an agreement between producer states on the allocation of agreed quotas is provided by the principle of sustainable utilization. There is a scientific basis for determining the maximum allowable offtake of ivory consistent with the maintenance of existing stocks of elephants. Preliminary estimates by the Renewable Resource Assessment Group, Imperial College London, indicate that such off-takes would aggregate to about 50 tonnes of ivory per annum, given present stocks of elephants.

Third, the basis for the provision of an external enforcement mechanism for the producers' agreement lies in the consumer states' interest in the maintenance of sustainable stocks of elephants, and also a sustainable flow of ivory. This consumers' agreement must take two specific forms. The consumer states must support the agreement by making purchases within its context, thus supporting a price for ivory far above the competitive price. Just as important, they must invest significant sums into the protection of the integrity of the system; they must make substantial efforts to restrict imports solely to ivory from within the system. The compensation which these states receive is the observable contribution of these efforts to the conservation of African elephant stocks.

Fourth, the combination of increased prices from reduced flows results in an increased expected return from standing stocks of elephants, thus increasing the incentives to invest in the maintenance of these stocks. The differential between the price of poached ivory and the price of certified ivory will then be equivalent to the expected riskiness of smuggling ivory into the points of final consumption. Thus, the poachers' prices may not increase so much if consumer states invest in significant ivory-monitoring efforts.[9]

We recommend the adoption of an Ivory Exchange mechanism (see p. 125). The essential purpose of an Exchange is the segregation of high-quality producers from low-quality producers for the benefit of an unknowing public, i.e. the ivory consumers. In this instance, the role of the Exchange is to determine which producers are placing ivory on the market from stable and well-managed populations. By accepting ivory from a producer, the Exchange itself certifies the ivory as flowing from well-managed stock.

An Exchange also acts to assure that counterfeiting is very difficult to achieve. That is, the centralized nature of this institution ensures that there is little possibility of confusing certificated and non-certificated ivory. All ivory must be brought to the Exchange for sale, and it is there marked and transferred directly to the purchasing state. No ivory in trade is legal unless it enters on a pre-announced shipment which moves directly from the Exchange to the importing state.[10]

One of the primary virtues of the Exchange would be its proximity to the elephant populations. The Exchange should be located in an African range state and membership should be likewise restricted. This enforces the incentives to develop this value of the resource by discouraging the intervention of non-producer objectives. In addition, this removes the factor of future uncertainties due to excessive reliance on external beneficience; the only actions which non-producers must take in this scenario are in their own self-interest. Thus, the Exchange operates by reinforcing the producers' incentives to invest in the resource in order to meet existing demand – a relatively reliable source of funding compared to foreign aid budgets.

In this way, the Ivory Exchange would be able to operate as an effective system of international regulation. It would both bolster incentives to invest while being substantially enforceable. It is the scheme of international regulation which is most likely to increase sustainable elephant populations.

Domestic Reform: The Importance of Local Ownership

The most cost-effective means of conserving elephant stocks would in fact occur through the mechanism of effective domestic management programmes; international regulation is a poor substitute for effective domestic regimes in regard to a species such as the elephant. It was argued in Chapter 5 that effective state management hinges crucially on improving the incentives of local communities to participate in the conservation of elephant and wildlife resources. This section elaborates on that theme.

The ultimate aim of community-based wildlife utilization is to improve the cooperation of local communities to participate in the conservation of elephant and wildlife resources. The rationale is simple: local people are the most familiar with the area and the wildlife within it; the failure to ensure their cooperation will make them indifferent and perhaps hostile to conservation efforts which they see as being imposed from outside. What is more, most communities claim a traditional right to exploit their own local wildlife resources. Hunting wildlife for meat is one of the most important of these rights, not only because the meat may be the only source of supplemental protein but also because hunting is a culturally significant craft, often with mystical links to tribal ancestors. Local hunters in the community have an important social function and status.[11]

The suppression of a community's rights to some exploitation of the local wildlife, or to a share in any of the proceeds resulting from wildlife utilization, may actually encourage local people to hunt illegally or to support outsiders engaged in these activities. In particular, illegal hunting for meat may become widespread for poorer communities or in areas where livestock rearing is difficult (e.g. due to tsetse fly infestation). The alienation of communities from their local wildlife may lead to direct conflicts. Large migratory animals like the elephant may increasingly be seen as a costly nuisance, inflicting extensive crop damage and occupying potentially arable land. Local communities may view elephant conservation as asking them to put up with these costs, with little benefit to themselves or compensation in return.

The history of wildlife conservation efforts in Africa has been dominated by a universal approach of divorcing local communities from any control or rights of exploitation of their wildlife, coupled with law enforcement efforts by the central and local authorities (notably the national parks and wildlife departments) to protect the wildlife.[12] Wildlife utilization, except perhaps for tourism and limited safari hunting, has been discouraged, and any safari and tourist revenues have gone to the state, not to local communities. The state's objective is to manage elephants and other wildlife for the benefit of the whole nation, whereas the local communities are denied access to protected areas and even to the right to hunt in areas neighboring them. The incentives for the local population to engage in or assist in poaching increase, while their incentives to cooperate in reducing poaching or aiding conservation efforts decrease. With the African elephant population declining rapidly, this strategy now needs urgent rethinking.

In Chapter 1, it was pointed out that one strong argument for elephant conservation is that it would permit a sustainable offtake of revenue from harvesting the resource (ivory, hide and meat) and from its non-consumptive economic value (tourism). Sustainable management of elephant populations may be able to generate substantial revenues, particularly if not just *one* economic use (e.g. ivory alone) but *several* can be made from elephants.

For example, a wildlife utilization study in Tanzania has emphasized the combined value of elephants: they are the prime attraction for tourists in the national parks (total tourist revenues are currently $25 million annually, with a large potential to expand); they are a key animal for safari hunting (a good trophy animal might be worth up to $20,000); and if populations recover sufficiently, they might be used for cropping for ivory, skin and meat (the illegal ivory trade is estimated at $10 million annually, with the loss of around 10,000 elephants; illegal meat hunting is worth around $40–50 million annually).[13]

It may be possible to design an elephant management strategy that obtains maximum revenue from both consumptive and non-consumptive uses. For example, in Botswana, a preliminary analysis

Table 6.1: **Economics benefits of different elephant management options, Botswana**

| | Net present value @ 6% (million pula, 1989) | | |
Option	After 5 years	After 10 years	After 15 years
1. Game Viewing with No Consumptive Uses	34.7	98.1	160.6
2. Game Viewing with Elephant Cropping	91.2	198.4	288.9
Difference (2-1)	56.5	100.3	128.3
Net Benefits from Consumptive Uses *a/*	60.0	110.1	144.4

Notes: *a/* The difference between options 1 and 2 is only an approximate indicator of the net benefits from consumptive uses, as the introduction of elephant cropping reduces the benefits from game-viewing tourism by 10 per cent. By allowing for this reduction, the net benefits from consumptive uses can be calculated.

Source: John Barnes, Department of Wildlife and National Parks, Botswana.

of the economic benefits for management of the elephant population compared the benefits from game viewing only to those involving viewing combined with some sustainable consumptive uses (see Table 6.1). The introduction of consumptive uses reduces the benefits from game-viewing tourism by 10 per cent, but results in additional benefits in forward linkages with tanning/processing of elephant hides, ivory carving and meat for crocodile farming. These additional benefits from consumptive uses almost double the total economic value of elephant populations.

The significant revenues that can be earned from consumptive and non-consumptive uses of African elephant populations suggest that these revenues are sufficient to allow at least some to be returned to local communities, with important consequences for reversing the current disincentives for these communities to engage in elephant conservation.

Several experiments have been underway in Africa which attempt to establish community-based wildlife utilization initiatives. The previous chapter mentioned the example of Communal Area Management Programmes for Indigenous Resources (CAMPFIRE) in Zimbabwe, where communities get direct revenue from the proceeds of wildlife utilization in their area. However, the elephant management problem in Zimbabwe has some distinct features. First, elephant culling has been undertaken since 1965, with the objective of managing elephant populations which are too great for their available range. Ivory sales from culling (plus confiscated illegal ivory) are essentially a by-product of this policy, the revenues of which both pay for the national management programmes and essentially compensate local communities for elephant damage, thus ensuring their cooperation in conservation. For example, adequate protection of elephant from illegal hunting is estimated to require recurrent expenditure annually of $200 per km². Despite some problems with poaching, it is estimated that the current elephant density in Zimbabwe of 0.7–1.0 elephants per km² is still too high. It is estimated that elephant densities should be reduced to less than 0.5 per km² over the present elephant range to ensure that vegetation loss due to elephant damage is not unsustainable.[14]

Thus, elephant management in Zimbabwe is concerned with reducing elephant populations, not increasing them; ivory sales are a necessary source of revenue for this management programme and for anti-poaching activities (which essentially protect the rents available to the state from this revenue). CAMPFIRE provides incentives for local communities both to co-exist with elephant populations and to discourage them from aiding or engaging in poaching. It is not surprising that other African states, notably Botswana, that have similar problems of elephant over-population for the available range area, are seriously considering developing the management model offered by Zimbabwe, including CAMPFIRE.

Whether a CAMPFIRE-like approach can be modified for the more standard elephant management problem throughout Africa – that is, elephant populations decimated by illegal hunting in the absence of any previous adequate management efforts – remains to be seem. Two illustrative examples are in Zambia: the Luangwa Integrated Resource Development Project (LIRDP) and the Administrative Design for the Management (ADMADE) of Game Management Areas (GMAs), both of which grew out of the Lupande Development Project (1985–7) in the Luangwa Valley.

ADMADE is strictly a wildlife utilization programme operating in the Lower Lupande hunting block, with replications beginning in 15 of the remaining 31 GMAs throughout Zambia. LIRDP is, in contrast, supposed to be a multi-sectoral programme for economic development, covering the South Luangwa National Park and the entire Lupande GMA (c. 35,000 people).[15] Although in addition to wildlife management LIRDP includes programmes in agriculture, forestry, fisheries, water resources and infrastructure, in practice, revenues are virtually dependent on wildlife utilization (currently 60 per cent of total), and 50 per cent of this is principally in the form of safari fees. Other sources of wildlife revenue include park entry fees and guard charges for tour companies, resident hunting permits and sales of meat and other products from culling schemes. ADMADE can obtain revenues from safari hunting fees, any culling schemes and local right-to-hunt fees, but not district or national hunting licenses.

Both schemes involve a revolving fund, whereby a proportion of revenues are returned to the local communities. Under ADMADE, 35 per cent of revenues are disbursed to community projects within the GMA; 40 per cent to wildlife management and enforcement programmes within the GMA, mainly the Village Scout Programmes; 15 per cent to National Park management; and 10 per cent to the Zambia National Tourist Board. Local employment is directly generated through the Village Scout Programmes and any culling operations, and indirectly through community projects. Local communities have access to meat from culling and from right-to-hunt fees. Under LIRDP, 40 per cent of revenues go to community projects in the Lupande GMA, selected by a Local Leaders' Sub-committee, and 60 per cent are for LIRDP project management and operating costs. LIRDP generates similar employment and consumption benefits to those of ADMADE. In addition, the LLS decides the allocation of offtake quotas for each wildlife species, ensuring that district game licenses for local hunting are equally divided among the six GMA chieftainships.

Currently, neither ADMADE nor LIRDP allow culling or hunting of elephants. Yet success in elephant conservation and the reduction of poaching has been claimed by both programmes. In the South Luangwa National Park and its adjacent GMAs, a 40 per cent decrease in elephant populations occurred from 1979 to 1985 – principally from illegal hunting. However, the number of elephant carcasses found in a 55 km^2 monitoring zone in Lower Lupande has declined from 0.09 per km^2 in 1985 to 0.01 in 1987–8, whereas elephant density has increased from 0.07 per km^2 to nearly 2.[16] LIRDP reports close to 500 illegal hunting arrests and nearly 400 firearms confiscated, with much assistance from local communities in aiding enquiries into illegal hunting activities.[17]

As both ADMADE and LIRDP operate in the same area

(Luangwa Valley), it is difficult to tell which programme is having an impact on reduced elephant poaching; it is also too early to tell which should be the more relevant model for replication – not just in Zambia but elsewhere in Africa where elephants are threatened.[18]

Conclusion: The Future of the African Elephant

The elephant has lived a long and noble existence on the plains and in the forests of Africa. Its range once included most of the European, Asian and American land masses, but now only two species remain and the African elephant is found in only 30 African states. Its numbers have been halving each decade since World War II, and in the 1980s this pace actually increased.

Attempts at discontinuing the slaughter are not new. For the past two decades African states have acted to ban the killing of elephants as well as the trade in ivory. International monitoring of the trade has existed for almost 15 years, and an attempt to control the trade has been in existence since 1986. All of these efforts have failed.

The singular outpouring of international concern over this species is remarkable nonetheless, because the situation of the elephant is not unique; it is an example of an extinction process that is afflicting a wide variety of the world's species. For example, the African elephant's decline mirrors that of its neighbour, the rhinoceros, which has been depleted in this same way to the point where only a few thousand of these animals now exist.

This concern must be turned to constructive effect, not just for the elephant, but for all endangered species. The choice in the past has often been between absolute domestication or absolute eradication. That is, as human uses of resources have intensified, wildlife has been forced to either "earn its keep" (as with the domestication of the Asian elephant) or to disappear altogether.

The purpose of a multi-faceted wildlife utilization strategy is to create a bridge between these two extremes. If it is possible to generate a flow of revenues from a wide and diverse range of wildlife uses (e.g. tourism, hide, meat and ivory), then it may be possible to avoid the domestication v. eradication dilemma.

The creation of a niche in this world for non-domesticated elephants depends crucially on the maximization of this aggregate value, and this depends in turn on the utilization of their ivory value. Obviously, the ivory trade has been doing the elephant great harm in the vast majority of the African range states; but, in a small minority of states, the trade has been rendering the elephant important benefits. Thus, the crucial causal factor in the elephant's decline has not been the ivory trade *per se*, but rather the failure of some states to utilize it constructively.

A long-term solution for the plight of many of these species must lie in a strategy of wildlife utilization developed in tandem with institutional reforms capable of constructively channelling human values into investment in wildlife.

The future of the African elephant is dependent upon the taking of immediate action. The ivory trade ban must be considered an interim measure, not a solution. Sustainable populations of the African elephant, as with so many other endangered species, will depend upon the development of reforms which constructively utilize the trade, rather than attempts to combat it. Institutional reforms to this end must be addressed now.

Notes

1. The states imposing unilateral ivory import bans prior to the CITES meeting were: Switzerland (13 June); Hong Kong (16 June); Canada (24 July); EEC (17 August); Australia (22 August); Taiwan (29 August).
2. Under the terms of USA law, ivory trophies should still be importable from Zimbabwe, Botswana and South Africa, but the US Fish and Wildlife Service has announced that it will require Appendix I import and export permits in the absence of these states accepting the Appendix I listing. The EEC has so far allowed trophy imports to continue from South Africa, Tanzania and Zimbabwe. It is uncertain how these import schemes will be implemented; both are currently under investigation by the respective authorities. Japan does not allow trophy imports.
3. The other African states with little tourist value deriving from elephants are those situated in central and western Africa. These states supported the Appendix I listing across the board. It is interesting to note that, within two weeks of the passage of the reservation deadline, the US Agency for International Development announced a debt forgiveness package totalling $300 million for a group of ten of these states.
4. The UK entered a reservation on behalf of Hong Kong; however, it has declared that this reservation is limited solely to exports of ivory to occur within the first six months of the ban.
5. Consistent with the intention to continue trade, India continued to declare its imports of ivory right up until the date of the ban, 18 January 1990. It is uncertain what the official position of India is now in regard to the continuation of the ivory trade.
6. See J. Caldwell and R. Luxmoore, "Recent Changes in World Ivory

Trade", World Conservation Monitoring Centre Report, (Cambridge, February 1990). The reports from the USA indicate that the worked ivory market "virtually collapsed in the second half of 1989" as a result of "consumer resistance". In Japan, retail prices of worked ivory have "risen steadily", with handseals now 12 per cent more than their 1989 prices and ivory for musical instruments actually doubling in price.

7. The trade in controlled drugs is the familiar example in the West, but in developing countries there is much greater experience with failed attempts at embargoes with regard to a broad range of substances. See J.N. Bhagwati (ed.), *Illegal Transactions in International Trade*, (North-Holland: Amsterdam, 1974); G. Hufbauer and J. Schott, *Economic Sanctions Reconsidered*, (Institute for International Economics, 1985).

8. Note from Chapter 1 that a substantial proportion of the global ivory trade has been geared to the tourist trade, perhaps as much as 25 per cent. These incidental purchases are almost impossible to detect and will very likely increase over previous quantities. Japanese customs officials have already detected some small-scale smuggling; for example, six persons were arrested in February 1990 for attempting to smuggle in 12,000 unfinished "name seals" from Taiwan. See J. Caldwell and R. Luxmoore, op. cit. (Note 6).

9. There has been observed a price differential between certificated ivory and non-certificated since the Management Quota System was put into place. It is likely that this prior differential related not to the costliness of smuggling, but rather to the costliness of purchased ivory documentation from African officials. At that time it was not necessary to engage in smuggling, since each range state had the unrestricted capacity to license the trade in other states' ivory by the sale of ivory documentation.

10. Efforts to monitor counterfeiting of exchange ivory will be helped by recent advances in isotope (microchemical) analysis to trace the origin of tusks. Microchemical differences in tusks may be sufficiently consistent for identifying the source of ivory against a library of reference samples. See R.H.V. Bell, J.P. Kelsall, M. Rawluk and D.H. Avery, "Tracing Ivory to Its Origin: Microchemical Evidence", *Pachyderm*, no. 12, (1989), pp. 29–31 and R. Lewin, "Ivory Signatures Trace the Origin of Tusks", *New Scientist*, (21 October 1989), p. 34.

11. For an extensive study of the cultural significance of local hunting see Stuart A. Marks, *The Imperial Lion*, (Westview Press: Boulder, Colorado, 1983).

12. See R.H.V. Bell and J.E. Clarke, "Funding and Financial Control" in R.H.V. Bell and E. McShane, *Wildlife Management in Africa*, (US Peace Corps: Washington DC, 1984); Nick Abel and Piers Blaikie, "Elephants, People, Parks and Development: The Case of Luangwa Valley, Zambia", *Environmental Management*, vol. 10, (1986), pp. 735–751; Dale M. Lewis, A.N. Mwenya and G.B. Kaweche, "African Solutions to Wildlife Problems in Africa: Insights from a Community-Based Project in Zambia", National Parks and Wildlife Services, Lupande, Zambia, (August 1989); Ministry of Lands, Natural Resources and Tourism,

Tanzania, in collaboration with International Trade Centre and IUCN, *Wildlife Utilisation in Tanzania*, ch. 7, (IUCN: Gland, Switzerland, October 1988); and Marks, op. cit. (Note 11).

13. *Wildlife Utilisation in Tanzania*, op. cit. (Note 12).

14. R.B. Martin, G.C. Craig and V.R. Booth (eds.), *Elephant Management in Zimbabwe*, Department of National Parks and Wild Life Management, Harare, Zimbabwe, (August 1989).

15. F.B. Lungo, "An Introduction to the Luangwa Integrated Resource Development Project, Zambia", Chipata Zambia, (September 1989); IUCN, *First Review Mission: Luangwa Integrated Resource Development Project*, (IUCN: Gland, Switzerland, October 1989); and Dale Lewis, "Zambia's Pragmatic Conservation Programme", *Pachyderm*, no. 12, (1989), pp. 24-6.

16. Lewis, *op. cit.* (Note 15).

17. LIRDP, "LIRDP Progress Report October 1988–September 1989, (Chipata, Zambia, September 1989).

18. For an independent assessment of LIRDP, and the need for the two programmes to cooperate to overcome administrative conflicts, see IUCN, op. cit. (Note 15).

INDEX

Edward B. Barbier is Director Designate of LEEC.

Joanne C. Burgess is Research Associate of LEEC.

Timothy M. Swanson is Lecturer in Law/Economics at UCL and Associate Fellow of LEEC.

David W. Pearce is Professor of Economics at UCL and Director of LEEC.